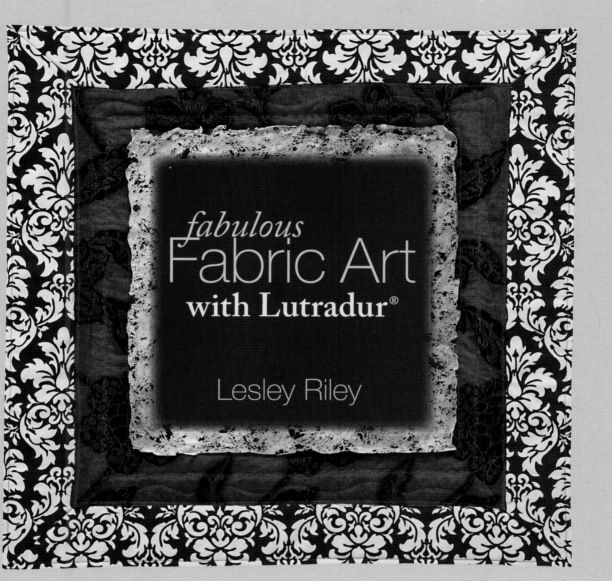

fabulous Fabric Art
with Lutradur®

Lesley Riley

For Quilting, Papercrafts, Mixed Media Art

27 Techniques & 14 Projects

Revolutionize Your Craft Experience!

C&T PUBLISHING

Text copyright © 2009 by Lesley Riley

Artwork copyright © 2009 by C&T Publishing, Inc.

PUBLISHER: *Amy Marson*

CREATIVE DIRECTOR: *Gailen Runge*

EDITORS: *Lynn Koolish and Cynthia Bix*

TECHNICAL EDITORS: *Carolyn Aune and Robyn Gronning*

COPYEDITOR/PROOFREADER: *Wordfirm Inc.*

COVER DESIGNER: *Kristy Zacharias*

BOOK DESIGNER: *Rose Sheifer-Wright*

PRODUCTION COORDINATOR: *Kirstie L. Pettersen*

ILLUSTRATOR: *Tim Manibusan*

PHOTOGRAPHY BY *Christina Carty-Francis and Diane Pedersen of C&T Publishing, Inc., unless otherwise noted*

Published by C&T Publishing, Inc., P.O. Box 1456, Lafayette, CA 94549

Library of Congress Cataloging-in-Publication Data

Riley, Lesley

  Fabulous fabric art with Lutradur : for quilting, papercrafts, mixed media art 27 techniques & 14 projects revolutionize your craft experience! / Lesley Riley.

    p. cm.

  Summary: "This book features 27 techniques and 14 projects using Lutradur for quilting, book arts, and multimedia. Pellon Lutradur is a cross between fabric and paper. You can stamp, paint, burn, sew, stencil, fold, and lightly iron it"--Provided by publisher.

  ISBN 978-1-57120-554-4 (paper trade : alk. paper)

  1. Handicraft. I. Title.

  TT157.R55 2009

  745.5--dc22

                                                    2008020480

Printed in China

10 9 8 7 6 5 4 3 2

Dedication

To my mother, who left us before she could hold this book in her hands. Thank you for a lifetime and beyond of your love. And to Lynn and Paul Simpson, you left us way too soon.

To my students—past, present, and future—you continually inspire me to find ways to bring the worlds of quilting and mixed media together.

Acknowledgments

To the four brave contributing artists who accepted my Lutradur challenge. I gave each artist two pieces of Lutradur—one to experiment with and one to create with—and no other guidance or instruction. Each person came up with beautiful results, uniquely their own. Thank you for lending your talents to my book.

To Judi Kauffman, who introduced me to Jan Grigsby and suggested we play ball.

To Jan Grigsby, who made the initial contact and got the ball rolling.

To Lynn Koolish, who helped me keep the ball in the air during the ins and outs of writing this book.

To Carolyn Aune, Cynthia Bix, Kristy Zacharias, and Rose Sheifer for making this book a home run.

Contents

Introduction

Writing a book is both fun and challenging. Each project sparks new ideas and discoveries, and the more you work, the more you think of projects and techniques that you just **must** include. It gets to the point when you (or your editors) have to say, "Stop! Enough! Or you'll never get the book turned in on time." It was especially true for this book on Lutradur, which is such a versatile material that I am still exploring and following all the lightbulbs that keep flashing in my head. But yes, I have to stop where I am and hand this over so that you, dear reader, can make your own discoveries with Lutradur.

What is Lutradur? Over the past few years, there has been quite a buzz over Lutradur among quilters, crafters, and mixed-media artists. Maybe you even have some of this material in your stash because, like me, you cannot resist the lure of buying the latest new thing. But there it sits, alone on a shelf, because you haven't yet figured out what to do with it.

Simply put, Lutradur is the magic in the middle—a versatile cross between fabric and paper. It has the body of paper and the strength of fabric. Unlike fabric, it will never fray or unravel. Lutradur is a 100% nonwoven polyester translucent web. Technically speaking, it is a thermally spun-bonded fabric, meaning the raw materials, some of which are cotton fibers, are melted and then spun through narrow jets to form endless fibers that are then stretched by hot air and laid into a web. Lutradur's open, airy structure absorbs paint, ink, image transfers, and more, creating a surface that filters light, yet has body and retains its shape. It is available in two weights: 70g, which is softer, lighter, and more flexible, and 100g, which is stiffer and good for books and direct printing. The majority of the projects in this book were made with 70g Lutradur.

Lutradur is thermoplastic, which means it changes when heated. It shrinks away and disappears when subjected to a heat gun or heat tool, producing the kind of organic and artistic effects that fiber and mixed-media artists love. It is an excellent surface to stitch, stamp, stencil, felt, and embellish.

I have been playing and experimenting with Lutradur for a few years and have discovered many techniques, tips, and tricks that I share with you in this book. As with any new material, exploring its potential is an ongoing process. It is my wish that you use this book for inspiration and reference. Let it be your guide for making your own discoveries and building on the ones I have presented here.

So where should you begin? Scan through 27 Things to Do with Lutradur (pages 6–26), and pick out the techniques that are familiar to you or the ones for which you already have the supplies. If you favor paper and mixed media, working with Lutradur is a good way to learn more about fabric. If you are fond of fabric, Lutradur is a good entry into the world of paper and mixed media. As you gain familiarity in working with Lutradur, I know you will be curious and eager to try other techniques and materials that may be new to you.

Note: Lutradur may perform like fabric, but it's not for wearing or sleeping under. Its stiff, durable, paperlike qualities make this sturdy fabric substitute too rough for comfort. As you will see, it is designed for art quilts, book arts, and mixed media.

Basic Tools and Supplies

Because Lutradur is so versatile and there are so many techniques you can use, you may think you have to go buy a lot of new supplies. The good news is that all the projects can be done with the most basic supplies, many of which you probably already have around your home. You can start experimenting, playing, and creating with these basic materials and save the fun extras for later, when you have a specific project in mind. For those of you (and you know who you are) who already have everything in your craft stash, Lutradur will give you the chance to use just about all of it!

If you have these basic tools and supplies, you're ready to start:

- **Scissors**
- **Ruler**
- **Paintbrushes**
- **Acrylic paint or inks**
- **Water container**
- **Glue**
- **Sewing machine or hand-sewing needle**
- **Thread**

Note: Refer to Resources (page 62) for sources of all supplies mentioned.

adding color and pattern

White Lutradur is a blank canvas begging for color and pattern. Color can be applied by using almost anything you have at hand: paint, inks, oil pastels, crayons, and markers. Experiment with what you have to see the various results. I enjoy using products like fluid acrylics, which leave the Lutradur somewhat transparent. If stronger color is needed, enhance selected areas with water-soluble oil pastels, opaque or metallic paints, or markers.

Paints

Acrylic paint is pigment suspended in an acrylic medium binder. To preserve Lutradur's translucency, I primarily use transparent acrylic paints, such as fluid acrylics, Dye-na-Flow, or Setacolor. Less transparent colors and opaque paints, especially metallics such as Lumiere and the Golden Fluid Iridescent colors, create beautiful rich color on Lutradur.

Lutradur is not as absorbent as natural fibers, yet it accepts color readily. If you wet it first, paints will blend and spread on their own. If you start with dry Lutradur, you can control the painted edge and color placement. The less water you use when painting, the stronger the color will be when the Lutradur dries. If the color is too light after the Lutradur dries, add more paint or some of the other coloring options described in this section.

Preparing to paint

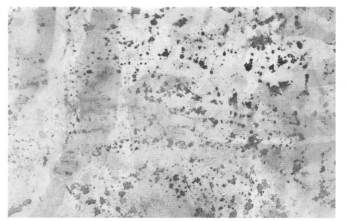

Lutradur painted with several colors and techniques

Inks

Most inks are made of dye, water, and helper chemicals. A dye usually reacts and bonds, temporarily or permanently, with the material it is applied to, whereas paint simply adheres and sits on top of the material as a layer. Dye inks, such as those made by Ranger, behave differently on Lutradur than paints do. The dye ink is attracted to and saturates the spun fibers, emphasizing Lutradur's webbed appearance. Acrylic inks, which are made of pigments, behave like paints on Lutradur.

Different paints and inks have different effects on Lutradur. Here's a sampling to give you some ideas.

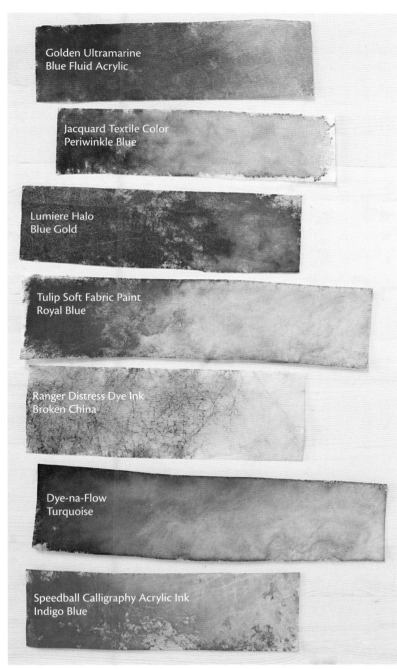

Golden Ultramarine
Blue Fluid Acrylic

Jacquard Textile Color
Periwinkle Blue

Lumiere Halo
Blue Gold

Tulip Soft Fabric Paint
Royal Blue

Ranger Distress Dye Ink
Broken China

Dye-na-Flow
Turquoise

Speedball Calligraphy Acrylic Ink
Indigo Blue

Paint and inks on Lutradur

Handling Wet Lutradur

Do not place very wet, painted Lutradur on an absorbent surface to dry. Some of the color could be drawn off the Lutradur onto your drying surface. Use plastic or place it on the lawn, which is my favorite method, weather permitting.

Double the Fun

When painting Lutradur, place other fabric, ribbon, paper, or lace under it. The paint that seeps through will create color-coordinated materials for you to use in your project or to add to your stash.

There's More Than One Way to Paint

Remember that adding color is not always done with a brush. Other techniques to try include scraping, sponging, spattering, spraying, lifting/blotting (with a paper towel), monoprinting, and so on.

PORTFOLIO OIL PASTELS

Applied to white Lutradur

Applied to white Lutradur and blended with water

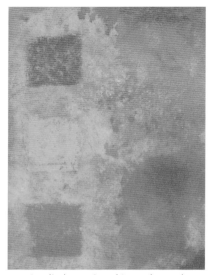

Applied to painted Lutradur and blended with water

Oil Pastels

One of my favorite ways of adding color to Lutradur is with Portfolio Oil Pastels. These versatile, water-soluble oil pastels are marketed for children, but they are a grown-up's best-kept secret for adding vibrant color to almost any surface. The secret is in the manufacturing of the water-soluble oil paint, which is formulated in a way that allows the oil paint to be mixed with water to form a workable paint that blends easily.

Portfolio Oil Pastels can be used to draw pictures or to color large areas. Apply these pastels dry and blend directly on the Lutradur, with or without water. Soft watercolor effects can be achieved by wetting the Lutradur before applying the oil pastels and using a wet brush to blend them after applying. You can also dip the pastel sticks in water and use them in the same way as Shiva Paintstiks.

Use Portfolio Oil Pastels to color white Lutradur or to enrich and deepen areas of color on painted Lutradur. After applying, let the oil pastels set for one to two days. Oil pastels can then be ironed to remove the oil and to set the paint. Place waxed paper or a paper towel over and under the design, and iron for a few seconds on a cotton setting.

Shiva Paintstiks are an oil-based, solvent-soluble paint in stick form that can be applied to Lutradur. Paintstiks should be left to dry for one day, then covered with newsprint to absorb any extra oils, and ironed to heat set the paint. Paint from Paintstiks should be applied last, because oil and water (or water-based media) don't mix.

Working with Oil Pastels and Crayons
When coloring and blending Lutradur with oil pastels and crayons, some of the webbing fibers will dislodge from the Lutradur. Just gather up the loose ends and pull them off.

Crayons

Caran d'Ache Neocolor and Metallic Artist Crayons are soft, water-resistant crayons that you can blend with a brush or your finger. They are soluble in turpentine and, as such, should not be used under any water-based materials, such as acrylic paints. Use these water-resistant crayons at the end of a project to heighten color or add accents.

Caran d'Ache Aquarelle water-soluble wax pastels perform similarly to Portfolio Oil Pastels when applied to Lutradur. Although they are more expensive than the oil pastels, these wax pastels come in a beautiful range of colors.

Familiar and easily available, crayons, such as Crayola, can also be used to apply color to Lutradur. Regular wax crayons will not blend but are great for drawing or enhancing areas with color.

Transfer Dyes

Lutradur is a synthetic material, and as such, it can only be dyed with disperse dyes, which are not very user friendly—except when used as transfer dyes. Disperse dyes for transfer dyeing can be purchased as crayons (Crayola Fabric Crayons) or transfer dye inks. These products are called transfer dyes because the dyes are applied to regular copy paper by drawing, stamping, stenciling, or painting and are then ironed onto Lutradur (or any other synthetic fabric). The dye colors don't look very exciting when they are on paper, but they will be transparent and bright after they are transferred.

Dye colors can be mixed on a palette before painting them onto paper, or they can be mixed while painting on the copy paper. Because they are transparent, dye colors can also be layered by ironing a second or third color over colors that have already been ironed onto Lutradur. Areas can also be masked out using paper stencils or other flat objects, such as leaves.

Left: Transfer dye colors,
Right: Color after ironing onto Lutradur

Transfer dye inks blended on copy paper and then ironed onto Lutradur

Transferring Dye Ink

1. Prepare your design by painting, stamping, or stenciling inks on copy paper. This is a transfer process; everything you create will be reversed after it is ironed onto your Lutradur. Be sure that any writing is backward on the paper so that it will come out correctly on the fabric. Let the ink dry.

2. Place the copy paper face down onto the Lutradur, and iron with a hot, dry iron to transfer the design or color.

Note: Don't confuse dye inks made for rubber stamping with transfer dye inks. Both will add color to Lutradur, but each in its own way.

Patinas

Patina is a naturally occurring oxidation process on metals. Sophisticated Finishes is a two-part patina solution available in craft and hardware stores that allows you to create real oxidation effects on surfaces other than metal, such as Lutradur. In a two-step process, you first apply the base paint, which contains real metallic particles that react to the patina solution, which you apply as the second step. You can actually create rust, verdigris, and other oxidized surfaces.

Top: Verdigris patina solution will oxidize on untreated Lutradur, creating permanent green color. Bottom: Rust patina

Use Lutradur that mimics rust, verdigris, and other patinaed metallic surfaces to add another dimension and texture to your projects. Follow the manufacturer's instructions to apply patina paints and solutions to Lutradur.

Faux patinas can be added to Lutradur with paint, embossing ink, and embossing powders, as seen in *RustyCrusty* (page 41). There are no specific proportions, rules, or restrictions. Rust or verdigris embossing powders, such as the ones from Ranger Ink (see Resources, page 62), do a great job of imitating the real thing and are fast and easy to use to create faux patinas. See the section on Embossing (page 20) or project directions for *RustyCrusty* (page 41) for specific instructions.

Stencils

Whether you are treating it like paper or fabric, Lutradur is a great surface for stenciling. Use commercially available stencils or create your own. To create your own stencils, draw, trace, or use your inkjet printer to create designs on Mylar, inkjet transparencies, or freezer paper. Cut out the design with an X-ACTO or craft knife.

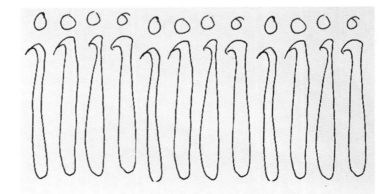

Freezer paper stencil ready to cut

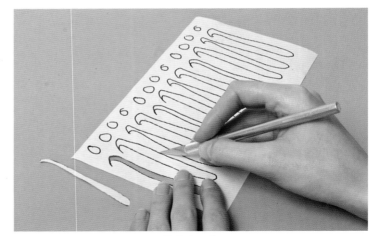

Cut stencil.

Freezer Paper Stencils

The advantages of using a freezer paper stencil are that it is easy to cut and you can iron the shiny side of the cut stencil directly onto your Lutradur. The disadvantage is that this type of stencil does not last very long.

Use a repositionable spray adhesive, such as Aleene's Spritz-On Reposition-It Tacky or Krylon Easy-Tack glue, on the back of a Mylar or transparency stencil to hold it in place while you do the actual stenciling. Use a foam brush or a stencil brush designed for fabric.

1. Place paint onto a palette or paper plate.

2. Dip the brush into the paint and tap off the excess.

3. Apply the paint directly into the open area of the stencil, using an up-and-down pouncing motion.

Apply paint with brush.

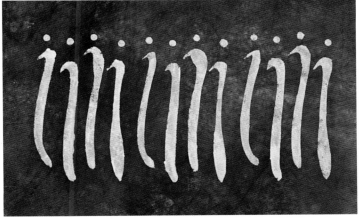

Completed stencil

Another stenciling method is to apply oil pastels or Shiva Paintstiks directly onto the Lutradur through the stencil. This direct application will give heavy solid areas of color. Softer effects can be achieved by first applying the stick color onto a palette, then loading a stencil brush with the color and applying it to the Lutradur with a gentle, circular motion. Experiment with blending colors and shading effects. When shading, start with the lighter color and add darker colors until you get the look you want.

Remember to heat set oil pastels and Shiva Paintstiks according to the manufacturer's instructions.

Stamps

Lutradur can be stamped using the same methods and materials you would use on paper or fabric. Lutradur behaves like fabric, so the stamped images will not be as bright and clear as they are on paper. Because of the open nature of Lutradur's bonded fibers, it is best to avoid using stamps that have a lot of detail. For the best results and for brighter colors, seal the Lutradur first with a coat of acrylic matte medium, or use paint rather than ink for stamping.

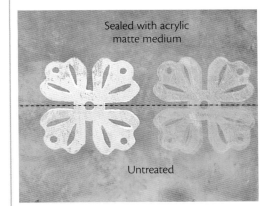

Sealed with acrylic matte medium

Untreated

Left side is stamped with white gesso. Right side is stamped with white StazOn rubber stamp ink. (Simply Foam stamp)

Stamping with Acrylic Paint

Stamping with acrylic paint will produce brighter, bolder imprints than will rubber stamp inks. Apply the paint to the stamp with a cosmetic sponge or foam brush.

Screening

Because it is stiffer than fabric but softer than paper, Lutradur is a good surface for screen prints using silkscreen, thermofax, or PhotoEZ screens. Use Versatex screen printing inks, or fluid or regular-bodied acrylics. If you are new to screen printing, several online tutorials and many excellent surface design books can help get you started. Refer to Resources (page 62) for screen printing resources.

Thermofax screen-printed Lutradur
using white gesso

printing and transferring

Printing

Lutradur is an excellent surface for computer printing. Lutradur, especially the heavier 100g weight, has enough body to go through most printers without using any paper backing. If you have a printer that uses pigment inks, no additional preparation is needed. For printers that use dye inks, which are water-based, you need to pretreat Lutradur with Bubble Jet Set or seal the Lutradur with PYM II (Preserve Your Memories), a light acrylic spray sealant, before and after printing to set the inks and prevent fading.

Because of the open, webbed structure of Lutradur, the printed images will not be as bright as those printed on paper or on a tightly woven fabric. The end result is similar to images printed onto a sheer fabric.

Treated with PYM II   Untreated

To print crisper, more color-saturated images, try one of two options: Either spray Lutradur with an acrylic sealant, such as PYM II (dry before printing), or coat the Lutradur with acrylic matte medium (dry before printing). For a colored background, save a step and tint the matte medium with acrylic paint or ink before coating the Lutradur. You can also print onto painted Lutradur; however, remember that the image will not be as bright as it is when printed onto white Lutradur.

High-contrast black-and-white images look great printed onto painted Lutradur.

Transferring

Image Transfers

Lutradur is an excellent surface for transfers made with photos printed from your inkjet printer. I use one of two methods, depending on the look I want. The first method uses Transfer Artist paper and an iron, giving perfect results every time. The other method uses inkjet printer transparencies and Golden Soft Gel acrylic medium (I prefer a matte finish, but glossy works just as well). Because Lutradur has a very open weave and is synthetic, most other transfer methods will not give the bright color and lasting results that these two methods do. Transferred images are much brighter and have better color saturation than do those printed directly onto Lutradur.

TRANSFERRED IMAGES

Printed on untreated Lutradur

Transferred from transparency using soft gel medium

Printed on Lutradur sealed with matte medium

Iron-on transfer with Transfer Artist paper

Printed onto Lutradur prepared with gesso

TRANSFER ARTIST PAPER TRANSFERS

Transfer Artist paper allows you to transfer photos from your inkjet printer. It works equally as well with dye-based and pigment printer inks. When the image is ironed onto almost any porous surface, it fuses with that surface. After the image is transferred, the material can be washed, stretched, reironed, bleached, painted, and even stitched over without damaging the image.

1. Print your photos onto a sheet of Transfer Artist paper. Group as many images as you can onto one sheet. Be sure to reverse or flip the image(s) before you print so that the result will look like the original. Use a plain paper setting, and set the printer to print between Draft and Best photo (available printer settings vary).

2. Cut out the image you want to transfer, trimming as closely to the image as possible.

3. Working on a lightly padded ironing board or on a hard surface such as Masonite, place the image face down on the Lutradur. Preheat your iron on the hottest setting, and iron the image, using some pressure for 10–30 seconds, depending on the size of the transfer. Be careful not to move the paper. Tape the image in place with electrical tape if desired (other tape adhesives will melt).

4. Cool to the touch before peeling paper off.

Drawing on Transfer Artist Paper

You can also draw an image or pattern onto Transfer Artist paper using markers, colored pencils, or crayons, and transfer it as you would a printed image.

TRANSPARENCIES AND GOLDEN ACRYLIC MEDIUM TRANSFERS

Images printed on inkjet printer transparencies can be transferred onto Lutradur using Golden Soft Gel medium and a burnisher. A burnisher is any hard, rounded surface used to rub, pushing the inks from the transparency to the Lutradur or other receiving surface. A spoon makes an excellent burnisher.

The results of this transfer method are not always perfect or guaranteed. Practice does make perfect, but with transfers, perfection isn't always the goal. That's what I like about the method—happy accidents, unpredictable results, and the timeworn appearance of the transferred image.

1. Print the selected images onto an inkjet transparency with your inkjet printer. Group as many images as you can onto one transparency. This is a transfer, so be sure to reverse or flip the image(s) before you print so that the result will look like the original. Remember, it is always necessary to reverse if there is text. Use a plain paper setting, and set the printer to print between Draft and Best photo (the available settings vary depending on the printer).

Using Transparencies

Transparencies have a specific side on which you need to print. This side is usually somewhat rougher or less slick than the wrong side. Read the manufacturer's instructions, and load the transparency into your printer according to your printer's instructions.

2. Cut out the image you want to transfer, and set it printed side down next to your work area.

3. Work on a smooth, flat, protected surface. Cover your work surface with wax paper or plastic, because the acrylic medium will seep through the Lutradur when it is applied. Using a foam brush, apply Golden Soft Gel medium onto the Lutradur, covering an area the size of your image. Use your finger to test for a smooth, even application of the medium. Your finger should glide easily over the surface, without becoming covered with gel medium. If there is white gel medium on your finger after testing the prepared area, you have applied too much. (Too much medium on the Lutradur will cause the inks to smear during burnishing.) With your finger, smooth out any brushstrokes, and continue to rub the medium into the Lutradur until you have a slick surface.

4. Place the inked side of the transparency onto the prepared Lutradur. The transparency should adhere to the surface. **Note:** If the surface is too wet, it will slide and smear.

5. Begin at the focal point, and work in a small circular motion, rubbing the surface with the back of a spoon or a rounded burnisher. Use enough pressure to push the inks off the transparency onto the Lutradur. You can apply more pressure in some areas for a full transfer, and less pressure in other areas for a softer effect.

6. Lift a corner of the transparency to check that everything has transferred to your liking. You can continue to burnish select areas and rub more, or, if the transfer is complete, you can remove the transparency from the Lutradur. If there was not enough medium or if the medium was not evenly applied, you may find that those areas did not transfer as well. Practice will eventually solve these problems.

Fixing Problem Spots

If you do not have enough medium on the Lutradur, the inks will not transfer. If after checking your transfer you see that there are white spots, try burnishing over these areas again before removing the transparency. If there is still no transfer, use a small brush to carefully add a bit more medium only to the untransferred area of the Lutradur; then burnish again.

7. After the transferred image is dry, you can trim it. You can also alter the surface of the Lutradur by zapping the untreated (no acrylic medium) areas with a heat gun to lace or distress (page 17); by adding more color with colored pencils, pastels, or paint; or by stitching, appliquéing, gluing, or collaging it.

Rub-on and Iron-on Transfers

Lutradur easily accepts all the commercial rub-on and iron-on transfers that you can now find in the scrapbook and fabric craft sections of your local stores or online shops. This type of transfer can quickly and easily add pattern, color, image, or even text to your Lutradur project.

Rub-on transfer by Basic Grey

Iron-on transfer by Me and My Big Ideas

Newsprint transfer on Lutradur, painted with fluid acrylic

Newsprint Transfers

Newsprint transfer is something I discovered through a happy accident! I placed some gel-medium-covered Lutradur on newspaper for a moment. When I lifted it, a thin layer of the newsprint had transferred to the Lutradur. The resulting piece became a wonderful addition to a collage.

1. Brush soft gel medium onto a piece of white or painted Lutradur. Place it on a piece of newspaper, and burnish to ensure complete contact with the newsprint.

2. Wait about 30 seconds; then lift the Lutradur from the newspaper. A very thin layer of newsprint should be adhered. If there is no transfer, reburnish and wait a bit longer before removing. Do not let the Lutradur dry on the newspaper. When the transferred newsprint is dry, it is ready for more color, stitching, or whatever you desire. Remember that you will get a mirror image of the print.

adding and subtracting

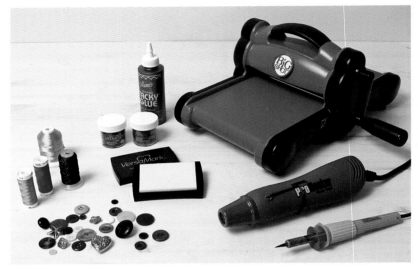

Stitching

Lutradur is the perfect surface for your hand and machine stitching ideas. The weight of the Lutradur makes it the perfect support for heavy applications, such as buttons and beads, as well as for delicate hand embroidery. Because Lutradur is an interfacing, it is also an excellent support for machine embroidery and decorative stitches.

Machine-stitched, hand-beaded Lutradur

Lutradur can be pieced and appliquéd into and onto quilts by hand or machine. Because it is rather stiff and scratchy, it is not recommended for bed quilts. However, Lutradur is very versatile for use in wall and art quilts. It makes great appliqués because cut edges do not ravel. Stitching can be added at any point in the process—before or after painting, distressing, collaging, transferring, and so on.

Transfer Artist transfer on Lutradur
pieced into quilt block

Hand Sewing with Lutradur
Use a large knot for hand sewing so it
won't slip through Lutradur's loose fibers.

Collaging

To make a collage, take bits and pieces of different materials and combine them into one work of art. Lutradur can be the base or background, the supporting cast, or the main character of a composition. A successful collage consists of overlapping and positioning elements that display a variety of contrasts— in size, color, texture, and positioning. I'll share a few ideas with you to help you get those creative juices flowing:

- Use painted Lutradur as a sturdy support for your paper or fabric layers.
- Create a machine- or hand-stitched fabric collage on Lutradur.
- Combine paper, fabric, stitching, and glue on painted, printed, stamped, or screened Lutradur.
- Cut out shapes, using stamped or printed images, from Lutradur to use in your collages.
- Create a dimensional collage by manipulating Lutradur after a collage is complete.

Lutradur and paper collage

Amount of lacing increases from left to right. Notice how Lutradur shrinks with more heat and lacing.

What to Do to Prevent the Lacing Effect

A heavy or thick application of paint, acrylic medium, or embossing powder will act as a resist, barrier, or mask to the heat, thus preventing lacing.

Laced and beaded Lutradur

Lacing

Lutradur disintegrates when subjected to high heat—use this to your advantage! Use a heat gun to selectively dissolve areas, producing an organic lace effect. Lutradur disappears quickly if overheated, so be sure to do a few test pieces before you work on your actual project.

 Under normal use, the heat from an iron is not sufficient to melt Lutradur. It takes the high, concentrated heat from a heat gun or heat tool.

The more heat you apply, the more the Lutradur will shrink, stiffen, and curl before it melts and disappears entirely. If you need your finished piece to be flatter and somewhat softer, you can iron it after lacing.

Burning

You can melt, singe, carve, or cut into Lutradur with a heat tool or soldering iron to create artistic cutouts, decorative edges, and free-form organic shapes. I use the Creative Textile Tool by Walnut Hollow, which comes with a pencil tip for general use and a mini-flow tip that works for burning the most delicate shapes and writing. The tool includes a handy on/off switch and a rest stand for the hot tip when the tool is not in use.

Burn edges and designs on painted Lutradur with Creative Textile Tool. Clean tip on a wood block.

The back of a cookie sheet or a smooth, glazed ceramic tile make great heat-safe work surfaces for drawing and burning shapes or words into Lutradur.

Safety first! There is no residue or ash when you burn Lutradur. Although Lutradur is non-toxic, you should still work in a well-ventilated area. Use precaution when working with a heat tool so you do not burn yourself or any area that may come in contact with the hot tool tip. This includes being careful with the cord—protect the cord so that it will not catch on anything (or anyone), causing the hot tool to fall from your work surface.

1. Lightly draw on the Lutradur the shapes, writing, or areas you wish to burn out. Use your drawing as a guide while burning. Or you can work freehand, designing or sketching as you go. Remember to leave breaks and create connectors, just as you would when cutting a stencil, so that your letter O, for example, does not become a big hole.

2. Plug in and turn on your heat tool. Let it heat up before you begin to work on the Lutradur. Rest the tip on a stand or protected surface, such as a ceramic tile or a small block of wood.

3. When working on the interior of the Lutradur, place the tool tip where you wish to burn. (I use the tapered point tip for this purpose.) If working along the edge of the Lutradur, use the side of the tool tip. Keep in mind that when the tool is completely heated, burning will be instantaneous. Therefore, you should work on a practice piece until you feel comfortable and in control.

Making Decorative Holes

Tiny decorative holes can be created by lightly and quickly touching the tip of the textile tool to the Lutradur. Be sure to hold the tool at a 90° angle to get perfect circles.

4. As you work, residue will begin to build up on the tool tip. If you see a charred look on your burned edges, clean the hot tip by scraping and rubbing it along the edge of a scrap block of wood. When you are finished, or before the next time you burn Lutradur, clean the cold tip by rubbing it with steel wool.

Negative shapes created by burning Lutradur

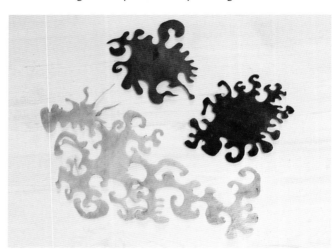

Positive shapes created by burning Lutradur

Burning Lutradur with a Flame

Burning Lutradur can also be done with a real flame from a candle, torch, or gas stove. Hold the Lutradur with kitchen tongs, and work over or next to a sink or bucket of water in a safe, controlled area. Although with a real flame, you don't have the control that you do when using a heat tool, this technique does work in a pinch.

Gluing and Fusing
Gluing

Some glues work better than others when gluing Lutradur—and some do not work at all. Choose your glue based on what you will glue the Lutradur to. Refer to the chart on the facing page for recommendations.

GLUING LUTRADUR TO:

GLUE:	LUTRADUR	FABRIC	PAPER	LIGHTWEIGHT OBJECTS TO LUTRADUR
Elmer's Glue	Poor Too wet No adhesion	Average Wets fabric	Good Quick adhesion	Good Slow to dry, but strong adhesion
Golden Soft Gel Medium	Good Instant adhesion	Good Adheres well	Good Quick adhesion	Poor
Aleene's Tacky Glue	Good Instant adhesion Softest when dry	Average Hard to spread but good adhesion Soft after drying	Good Quick adhesion	Good Quick adhesion Fast drying
Diamond Glaze	Poor Too wet Dries yellow	Good Adheres well	Good Quick adhesion	Good Quick adhesion Fast drying
Aleene's Fast Grab	Poor No adhesion	Good Easy to spread Adheres well	Good Quick adhesion	Good Instant hold Average drying
Aleene's Fabric Fusion	Poor No adhesion	Good Easy to spread Adheres well	Good Quick adhesion	Poor No adhesion

Fusing

Fusing Lutradur is one way to adhere it to a quilt or collage surface. Although Lutradur dissolves when exposed to heat, it is still possible to fuse it because the iron temperature required for iron-on fusibles is not hot enough to pose a problem. Any brand of fusible web will work; simply follow the manufacturer's instructions. I prefer Wonder-Under because it is lightweight. In addition, I can use it on its paper backing or remove pieces of it from the paper backing and insert it between two surfaces to tack things in place before machine stitching.

Another fusing method particular to Lutradur is to fuse two pieces together with the heat tool, creating a double-sided piece.

1. Choose two contrasting colors of Lutradur.

2. Burn designs in the piece that will become the top.

3. Place the burned piece onto the contrasting piece of Lutradur and burn or cut a shape along the outside edges. The 2 layers will fuse at the edges as the heat tool cuts the shape. You can also work with 3 layers and sandwich a solid color between 2 pieces of Lutradur that already have shapes or designs burned into them. You then fuse the 3 layers together.

Two pieces of Lutradur fuse together at edges when cut with heat tool.

Embossing

Embossing powders are fine-grained particles that melt when heat is applied, leaving a raised surface or design. The powders are held in place by preparing the surface with something wet, such as a rubber stamp pigment inkpad (pigment inks take longer to dry than do dye inks) or paint. The powder will adhere to the wet surface. Shake off the excess embossing powder, and then heat the area with a heat gun to melt the powders and to emboss the surface.

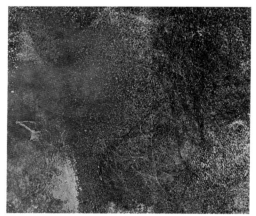

Embossed Lutradur

Even though Lutradur disappears when it is subjected to the high heat of a heat gun, you can still emboss on Lutradur. Here's the trick: Work quickly and from a distance.

1. After you have applied the embossing powder to the Lutradur and shaken off the excess, but before you emboss, preheat the heat gun by holding it away from the Lutradur for about 10 seconds.

2. When the heat gun is hot, use it in a rapid up-and-down motion, holding it no closer than 4–5 inches from the Lutradur for no more than 3 seconds at a time. If you see the Lutradur start to buckle before the embossing powder has cured, you are holding the tool too close to the Lutradur or holding it close for too long. If some disintegration of the Lutradur occurs, accept it as a happy accident.

What to Do with Buckled Lutradur

Although you can flatten Lutradur that has buckled from the high heat of a heat gun by ironing it, you cannot iron embossed Lutradur. If you do, the embossing powder will remelt and stick to your iron or pressing cloth.

Lutradur can also handle the kind of embossing where you create a raised surface on paper through pressure and the use of an embossing plate. The Cuttlebug is a small craft machine that creates embossed designs on Lutradur, paper, and some fabrics; it also die-cuts all of the above.

Die-Cutting and Punching

Because Lutradur behaves like paper, it is an excellent material for decorative punching or die-cuts. A die-cut is a shaped cutter through which material, such as plastic, paper, paper-backed fabric, or Lutradur, is pressed to create desired shapes. The simplest method is to use a handheld punch. Next in line are the home and personal use machines, such as the Sizzix, Quickutz, or Cricut systems, for cutting small shapes and alphabets. High-tech systems, such as AccuCut, which have hundreds of possible patterns and dies in a variety of sizes, may be available for use at your local stamp/scrapbook store or quilt shop.

Painted die-cuts made using AccuCut

Because cut edges of Lutradur do not ravel or fray, it is possible to punch or die-cut very small or very intricate designs for your project. In addition, because of Lutradur's strength, there is no problem with tearing or ripping delicate edges.

1. Determine how much Lutradur you will need by figuring out what size sheet will fit into your die-cut machine and how many individual cuts or punches you can get from one sheet.

2. Prepare as many sheets as you will need with any painting or patterning that you desire.

3. To make the application of small or unwieldy die-cut shapes easier, spray the back with a repositionable adhesive, such as Aleene's Spritz-On

Reposition-It Tacky Glue or Krylon Easy-Tack glue. Another option is to iron paper-backed fusible web, such as Wonder-Under, to one side of the Lutradur **before** you cut or punch out any shapes. The die-cut shapes can then be ironed in place on your quilt or fabric project.

Using Die-Cut Machines
Die-cut machines and handheld punches can also be used to create stencils on Mylar and freezer paper.

Writing

The secret to writing on Lutradur is to write slowly and with a light hand. Because of the loose weave, your pen or marker may get caught in the fibers if you use too much pressure. The pen will tend to skip if you write too fast. A variety of pens and markers will work, but avoid very small or fine nibs. My advice is to get a scrap of Lutradur and test the pens you already have. Or you can take a scrap of Lutradur to the craft store and test their sample pens until you find a few you like.

Writing samples on Lutradur

Resists

Use acrylic medium or paint such as Golden Soft Gel medium, gesso, or craft paints as a permanent resist by stamping, painting, or screen printing an image or pattern on Lutradur before painting or distressing it. A resist seals the area of the Lutradur that it is

applied to and keeps both color and heat from penetrating the fibers. The thicker the paint or acrylic medium application, the more resistant it is to heat distressing. Note that washes of fluid paint on a sheet of Lutradur will still allow for heat distressing. Thicker layers, such as those you apply by stamp, stencil, or screen print, provide more of a barrier and resist the heat better.

Paint-stamped image (using a Simply Foam stamp) acts as resist to lacing.

You can also use a resist on painted Lutradur before adding another layer of paint. Stamp, stencil, screen print, or simply paint acrylic medium over painted Lutradur. When you apply a second layer of fluid paint, the base color will show through the areas that have been sealed with the acrylic resist.

Anything that blocks direct heat, such as fabric, can also act as a resist or barrier to the heat gun. The areas around the appliquéd images in *Oh the Places I've Been* (page 57) were distressed and laced with a heat gun. The Lutradur under the appliqués was not affected.

Reverse of *Oh the Places I've Been*: Fabric appliqués resist heat and prevent lacing.

Constructing

Lutradur's body and stiffness make it an excellent material for constructing three-dimensional objects. These qualities also help it hold its shape for weaving strips and for dimensional sewing techniques, such as pleats or folds. Think envelopes, vessels, boxes, containers, and freestanding sculpture.

- Construct boxes of any size from Lutradur by following the layout on page 29.
- Cut strips from painted Lutradur and weave them into flat or shaped constructions.
- Make tubular shapes by sewing or gluing the edges of Lutradur together.
- For a unique effect that curls on its own, sew small pleats into a sheet of Lutradur.

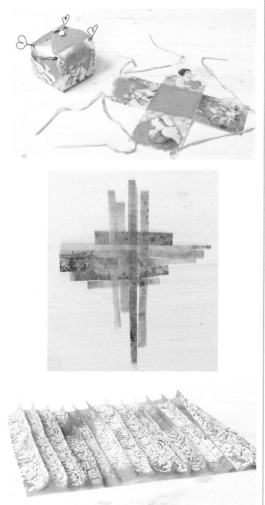

Boxes, weavings, and pleats constructed from Lutradur

Layering

Take advantage of Lutradur's translucency and its burn and lace effects by layering it over other surfaces, letting the bottom layer peek through the Lutradur.

Layered, laced and foiled Lutradur in *Angelic* (page 53)

Layering Lutradur over patterned fabric adds another dimension to Let's Play (page 55).

Use colored or patterned paper or fabric behind white, painted, or printed Lutradur in quilts and collages. There is usually enough translucence in Lutradur for layered effects, even without burning or lacing.

Lutradur will fuse to itself when you cut two or more layers with a heat tool. Any two (or more) edges that come into contact with the tip of the heat tool will fuse together. See Fusing (page 19) for details.

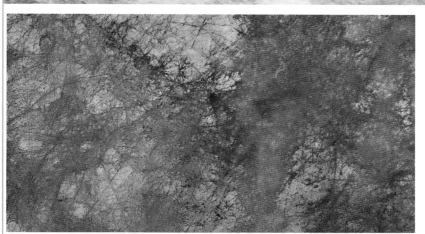

Rubbing

To cover both large and small areas of Lutradur with pattern and color, you can do rubbings over any reasonably flat surface with raised elements that are firm enough and thick enough for the texture to be felt through the Lutradur.

1. Place Lutradur over a dimensional surface, such as commercially available rubbing plates, screens, blocks, shapes constructed from twisted wire, cardboard wrapped with cording, and so on.

2. Use oil pastels or oil sticks to create rubbings onto painted or plain Lutradur, and let them dry.

3. Heat set with an iron, using a pressing cloth if necessary.

Left: Painted Lutradur
Right: Colors pop after sealing with matte medium.

combining materials

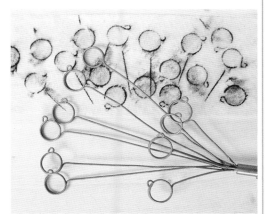

Rubbing created with Portfolio Oil Pastels over flattened metal shapes

Sealing

Working with Lutradur in its natural state is wonderful, but sometimes you may want to seal it with acrylic gel or medium:

- Seal before inkjet printing or stamping to create crisper, brighter images.
- Conserve paint by sealing Lutradur before applying paint.
- Seal with glossy medium to create a shiny appearance.
- Seal collaged Lutradur to protect the surface.
- Seal a painted surface to pop paint colors.

Angelina

What happens when you combine two synthetic, heat-fusible materials? Magic! Bond Angelina fibers or Angelina film (following the manufacturer's instructions) to a background of preprinted, painted, or decorated Lutradur. The thin layers of Angelina fibers will melt and bond into the Lutradur.

To create this effect, lay strands of Angelina fibers (you can mix colors together)—or a sheet or shapes cut from Angelina film—on top of white or painted Lutradur. Cover with a sheet of paper or baking parchment, and iron for a few seconds to fuse. Too much heat will take the shine from the fibers, so use a setting just below cotton on your iron. As when I cook, I work by smell. When I notice a smell, the fibers have bonded and I'm done.

Angelina fibers and film bonded
to painted Lutradur

You can also add other nonfusible items, such as yarn or other fibers, feathers, threads, or bits of fabric, between the layers of Angelina and Lutradur. Be sure to have several areas of direct contact between the Lutradur and the Angelina, as they will only bond to each other. The other materials will be trapped between them.

Foiling

Foiling Lutradur adds a bit of shine and sparkle to your projects. There are two methods for adhering foil to Lutradur: fusing, and gluing (including using dimensional adhesive).

Special Effect with Foil
To achieve a more random, hit-or-miss coverage with the foil, use the side edge of the iron to fuse the foil to selected areas.

Fusing Foil

1. Cut shapes or a sheet (for full coverage) from any paper-backed fusible web, such as Wonder-Under.

Materials

2. Iron the fusible web onto the Lutradur, following the fusible manufacturer's instructions.

3. Remove the paper from the fusible web in preparation for ironing the foil in place.

4. Cut a piece of foil slightly larger than the area to be covered. To create a broken or distressed appearance, crumple the foil before ironing.

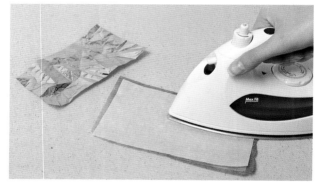
Iron fusible web to Lutradur.

5. Place the foil onto the fusible web, placing the foil **shiny side up**.

6. Preheat your iron to a cotton setting. Use the iron to bond the foil in place.

Iron foil, shiny side up, to fusible web.

7. Remove the foil when cool.

Foiling on Lutradur

Lutradur was painted blue, foiled using Wonder-Under, then laced with heat gun.

Gluing and Using Dimensional Adhesive

1. Use a paintbrush, stamp, stencil, or glue bottle nozzle to apply glue directly to the Lutradur. Wait at least 1 hour to allow the glue to dry until it is tacky. (In humid climates, this may take up to 2 hours.) For dimensional glue effects, apply the glue straight from the bottle nozzle to achieve a dimensional line. Let the glue dry until it is clear and rigid, but still tacky, so that when you apply the foil, the glue's dimensional effect is not flattened.

2. Place a piece of foil **shiny side up** over the glue.

3. Use the tip of your iron to burnish the foil. You can try rubbing the foil with your finger or a burnisher, such as the back of a spoon; if the glue is tacky enough, the foil will adhere.

4. Remove the foil sheet when cool.

5. Repeat the process if necessary to cover all the glue.

Using Foil Sheets
You can keep using a foil sheet over and over until all the foil has been removed from the sheet.

Add More Color
Paint fusible web using the same acrylic paints and inks you use on Lutradur. Apply it to web that is still on the paper backing, and when dry, iron the painted fusible web onto the Lutradur before foiling. This extra layer of color adds dimension and spark to the work.

Test Before Foiling
Because a hot iron can damage some foils, be sure to do a test run first. If necessary, iron with a cotton pressing cloth or Teflon sheet over the foil.

Needle Felting

Have you noticed that Lutradur is webbed? Those interlaced spun fibers that make up a sheet of Lutradur are exactly what you need for needle felting. You can do needle felting by hand, using a barbed hand-felting needle or multi-needle felting tool, or by machine, using a special attachment or a dedicated needle felting machine. Use these tools to push a top layer of wool into a base layer of Lutradur. The in-and-out motion of the felting needles interlocks the fibers.

Fibers, Clover hand needle felting tool, and
Clover needle felting mat for felting on painted Lutradur

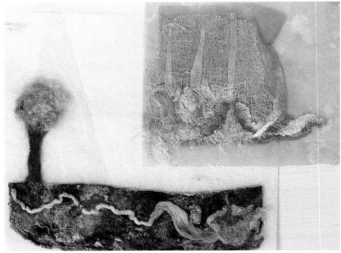

Two examples of machine needle-felted Lutradur

Handle Felting Needles with Care

Felting needles are barbed and very sharp! Avoid touching the ends with your fingers, and keep them out of reach of children and pets.

1. Decide what shape you would like your finished felt piece to take. You can felt unique shapes, such as circles or hearts, to appliqué to a quilt or to use as accents on artwork. Or you can create a pictorial piece, such as *Autumn Field* (page 59). Although you can cut out a shape beforehand, it is easier to draw on a rectangle of Lutradur, and then cut the shape to size after you have finished felting. It's important to give yourself excess Lutradur to hold onto while felting, so be sure to start larger than your desired finished size.

Finishing Felted Shapes

When you are finished felting specific shapes, leave a seam allowance when you cut it out. Fold the extra Lutradur toward the back to create a nice finished edge.

2. Gather an assortment of materials to felt to your Lutradur. You can use commercial felt, wool, wool roving, fleece, and yarn. Layer wool so that is about ¼˝ to ½˝ thick and at least ½˝ bigger on all sides than the shape template you've created.

3. If you are using a hand felting tool or individual needles, place the Lutradur on top of a piece of foam. Use a **straight** up-and-down motion, not an angle, to poke the wool, yarn, or other fiber into the Lutradur following a random pattern. You don't need to use a lot of force. If the felting gets too bulky, flip the Lutradur over, and felt from the other side. You may end up liking the reverse better!

Note: If you are using a needle felting machine, follow the manufacturer's instructions and precautions.

For More on Needle Felting

Find more information on needle felting in Fast, Fun & Easy Needle Felting: 8 Techniques & Projects—Creative Results in Minutes! by Lynne Farris, available from your local quilt or craft store, or C&T Publishing (Resources, page 62).

Baby's Blocks

Made by Lesley Riley

Finished sizes: 3″ × 3″, 2¼″ × 2¼″, 1½″ × 1½″

Techniques used: transferring (page 13), stitching (page 16), constructing (page 22)

With a new grandchild on the way, my mind is on babies. When I saw these new Ready-to-Go! Blank Board Blocks from C&T Publishing, I instantly envisioned them encased in Lutradur and patterned with letters and toys. I wanted a bright bold look, so I transferred the images rather than printing them directly onto the Lutradur, which would have created a softer, paler look. If you do not have a wide-carriage printer (I do not), transferring the images also enables you to create the larger blocks on one piece of Lutradur. By using a transparency transfer, you can also position each block accurately.

Use the template on page 29 to lay out each block. You could also create each side of a block separately and stitch them together, one by one, or even mix and match images on Lutradur with squares of fabric. With six sides to a block, imagine the possibilities. Hand stitching the edges closed creates a soft, hand-made finish and offers you the opportunity to have fun embellishing the blocks with beads and baubles—of course, those blocks wouldn't be for babies, but they're great for babes like us.

materials

See page 62 for sources of supplies.

- Lutradur: 2 pieces 8½" × 11" for 2 small blocks
    1 piece 11" × 13" for large block
- Ready-to-Go! Blank Board Blocks:
    1 block 3" × 3"
    1 block 2¼" × 2¼"
    1 block 1½" × 1½"
- Photo-editing computer software
- Inkjet transparency sheets
- Golden Soft Gel medium: matte
- 1" foam brush
- Burnisher
- Hand-sewing needle
- Embroidery thread or yarn
- Decorative yarns, charms, beads for embellishment (optional)

method

See pages 6–26 for techniques.

The box template on the facing page is the layout for creating a one-piece Lutradur cover for a 2¼" block. Follow the template to determine where you will place each image and to correctly orient each side so that the images will be right side up when the block is assembled. To make blocks in other sizes, create your own template in the same configuration. You need to add a ¹⁄₁₆" margin to each side of the template squares to allow for the block to be folded and stitched. For example, if you are covering the 3" block, each template square should measure 3⅛".

1. Use a pencil to draw around each square template on your Lutradur so you know where to place the transfers. Be sure you have added ¹⁄₁₆" seam allowance around each square.

2. For each block, prepare on your computer 3 images and 3 alphabet letters, a total of 6 block sides. Create alphabet letter blocks using your software program's text tool, or scan in letters from magazines or other resources. I also used the software to create the background color for the letters and images. Crop or scale each image to fit your block size.

3. Print the block images onto an inkjet transparency (page 14). **Remember to reverse the images before printing!**

4. The arrows on the template indicate the direction each image should be facing. Use that as a guide to transfer each square separately (page 29). After the Lutradur is dry, cut out the block cover, fold over the block, and stitch the open sides together.

TIP *Covers for the two smaller blocks can be printed directly onto one piece of Lutradur. After you have created an image for each side, arrange them on a new document, according to the template. Print onto an 8½" × 11" piece of Lutradur.*

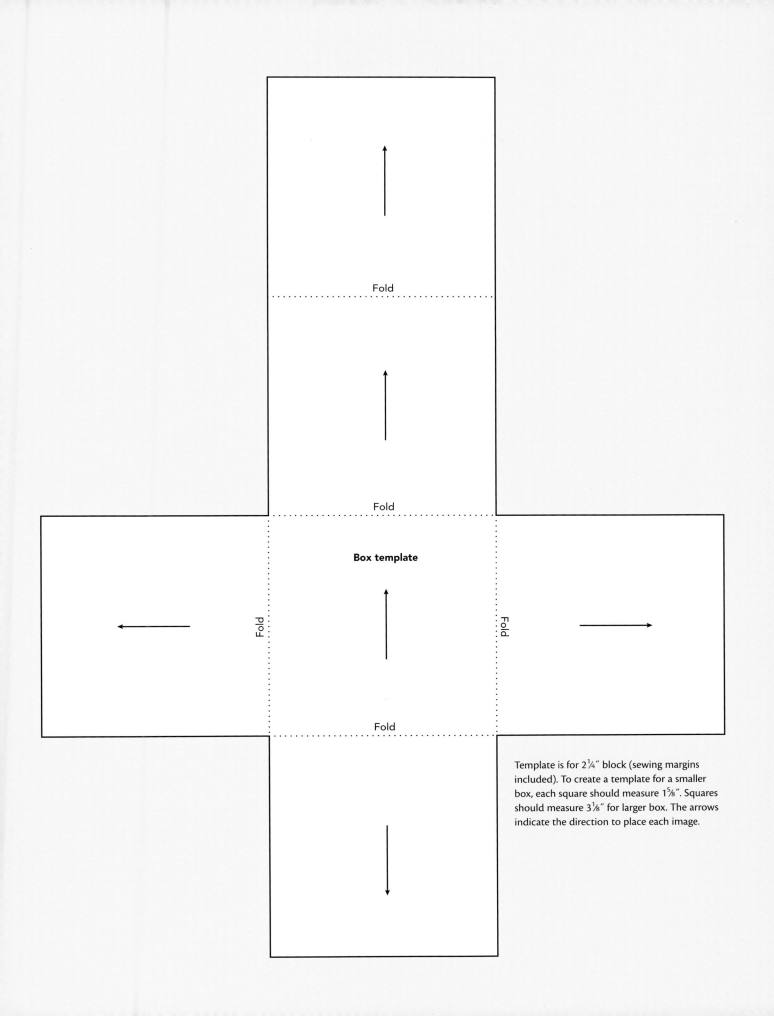

Fold

Fold

Fold

Box template

Fold

Fold

Fold

Template is for 2¼″ block (sewing margins included). To create a template for a smaller box, each square should measure 1⅝″. Squares should measure 3⅛″ for larger box. The arrows indicate the direction to place each image.

Her Heart

Made by Claudine Hellmuth

Finished size: 6″ × 6″

Techniques used: paints (page 6), embossing (page 20),
resists (page 21), collaging (page 16), gluing (page 18)

While learning to work with Lutradur, I wanted to incorporate it into a collage using gel medium, acrylic paints, pen, and ink. I was excited to see that the Lutradur took the paint wonderfully. I was able to paint on the Lutradur to create a stain effect. There are so many different things to do with this product—burning, shrinking, sewing. I am excited to experiment more!

—Claudine

materials

See page 62 for sources of supplies.

- Lutradur: 1 piece 8″ × 8″
- Embossing pen: clear
- UTEE (Ultra Thick Embossing Enamel) or embossing powder (clear)
- Golden Fluid acrylics
- Small, stretched canvas (for the project shown, I used a canvas 6″ × 6″)
- Collage papers and images
- Pens
- Glue
- Ribbon (approximately ¾ yard or enough to go around the canvas edge)
- Heat gun

method

See pages 6–26 for techniques.

1. Paint the canvas background with acrylic paint.

2. Draw on a piece of Lutradur with a clear embossing pen (this project has marks that look like grass). Sprinkle UTEE or clear embossing powder over your drawing, shake off the excess, and then emboss with a heat gun (page 20).

3. After the Lutradur is cool, paint it with watered-down acrylic paint (page 6). Make sure the paint is really watery, so it will look like a stain. The embossing powder creates a resist wherever you embossed, and the paint will not stick. Allow the Lutradur to dry.

4. Create a collage on the stretched canvas, using the Lutradur and your favorite papers and images (page 16). Draw design lines as needed.

5. Glue decorative ribbon around the canvas edge for a nice finished presentation.

 This technique could also be done using a clear embossing stamp pad and your favorite stamps.

CoCo Vin & Chickie Cheese

Made by Judi Kauffman

Finished size: 8″ × 9″

Techniques used: paints (page 6), constructing (page 22), gluing (page 18)

CoCo Vin and her chick appeared out of nowhere. On my work table, I had a wool felt cone, some felt die-cuts, and beads in a plastic bag that was sitting on top of the folded piece of Lutradur I had planned to paint that day. I took out the largest blue felt bead and cut it from one hole to the other to find out what was inside. Instantly, I saw a mouth. The elongated folk-style heart was folded to make lips, and the long tip stuck out so much that it became a beak—I had the head of a chicken in hand. The next thing I knew, I'd cut a three-petal section from a die-cut felt flower to make her comb. The two petals remaining looked about right for a chick's comb, so I took out a smaller felt bead and heart for the chick's head and beak, a die-cut felt dress, and another flower for her collar. Painted Lutradur became the feathers.

I like the stiffness and body of Lutradur, the way it takes color, and the fact that it doesn't fray. For this project, I only did the one thing—painted feathers. If you want to know what I plan to do next, here are two other thoughts: I envision working with folded, more structural projects—boxes and envelopes, perhaps. I also think it will be fun to sew onto the surface, in addition to altering it with paint and stamps.

—Judi

materials

See page 62 for sources of supplies.

- Lutradur: 1 piece 12″ × 12″
- Acrylic paint or dye inks: Copper, gold, bottle green, turquoise
- Wool felt cone 6″ high
- Felt beads: 1 piece approximately ¾″ diameter and 1 piece approximately 1¾″ diameter
- Die-cut felt flowers, heart, and dress
- Arm and hand charms
- Assorted fibers, tied in a loose bow
- Cat's eye stickers: 1 pair 5mm, 1 pair 7mm
- Glue: Beacon Kids Choice and Gem-Tac for eyes (recommended)
- Hand-sewing needle and thread
- Sponge dauber
- Stuffing: fiberfill, old stockings, or cotton balls (optional)

method

See pages 6–26 for techniques.

1. Paint Lutradur with acrylic paints or dye inks (pages 6–7), and let it dry.

2. Fold the painted Lutradur in half, and cut pairs of mirror-image feathers, some curved and some straight. (I cut approximately 12–14 pairs.)

3. Cut the backs of the felt beads flat so the heads can easily be glued in place.

4. Glue CoCo's and Chickie's beaks, eyes, and combs in place on the rounded side of the beads. Let the glue dry.

5. Glue CoCo's head in place. Glue Chickie's dress and collar in place, then her head and comb.

6. Sew Chickie's arms and CoCo's hands in place.

7. Glue the feathers in place, keeping them in mirror-image pairs and hiding the tip of the felt cone. Refer to the project photo on the facing page.

8. Stuff the cone. **Option:** Cut a piece of felt or fabric to fit inside the base of the cone. If you are using fabric, cut a slightly larger piece so that the raw edges can be turned under. Sew the felt or fabric in place to hold the stuffing inside.

Last Song of the Night

Made by Katie Kendrick

Finished size: 5½″ × 8″

Techniques used: transferring (page 13), paints (page 6), lacing (page 17),
layering (page 22), gluing (page 18), collaging (page 16)

My inspiration for this piece came from the beauty of the land and the variety of birds that inhabit the trees and brush where I live. The piece of old wood I used was once part of a tiny house that stood in the middle of an orchard 100 yards away from where our house stands. I collected a pile of the old boards and shingles after the building was demolished. I love to incorporate those rustic pieces into my work when I can.

Lutradur's translucent nature, coupled with its mesh quality, made it an interesting fabric to work with. It is very strong and tough, yet it looks delicate; no amount of abuse I dished out through my altering and layering damaged it in any way. This was my first exposure to Lutradur. By the time I finished the project, I ordered 2 yards of it so that I could continue playing and experimenting with it on my own.

—Katie

materials

See page 62 for sources of supplies.

- Lutradur: 1 piece 6″ × 9″, 1 piece 3″ × 5″
- Mica: 1 piece 3″ × 4″
- Inkjet transparency sheets
- Golden Soft Gel medium
- Golden Fluid acrylics: Cobalt Turquoise with a dash of Cerulean Blue Deep
- Vintage papers
- Ranger Distress ink: Pine Needles
- Wood scrap: 1 piece 5½″ × 8″
- Bits found in the woods for embellishment
- Nails
- Glue (for gluing the paper to the Lutradur)
- Lemon juice
- Rubbing alcohol
- Heat gun
- Sewing machine

method

See pages 6–26 for techniques.

1. Print an image onto a transparency, and use soft gel medium to transfer it to the smaller Lutradur piece (page 14). Let it dry. Paint over the transferred image with watered-down fluid acrylics. While the paint is wet, splash on drops of rubbing alcohol for a mottled effect. Let it dry.

2. Paint the large Lutradur piece with fluid acrylics (page 6). Let it dry. Lace and distress the edges of the larger piece with a heat gun to create a frame for the image (page 17).

3. Cut a piece of vintage paper to the desired size to create a background for the image. Distress the paper using distress ink (follow the manufacturer's instructions). Cut another smaller piece of paper to place behind the transferred image, creating a layered effect with text peeking through. Sprinkle lemon juice on the paper, then age and distress it with a heat gun.

4. Machine stitch the piece of mica onto the transferred image. Glue the smaller paper to the back of the image.

5. Glue the large paper to the back of the distressed Lutradur frame. Glue the image layers on top.

6. Nail the Lutradur to the scrap of wood. Add additional found embellishments as desired.

Squared Away

Made by Jenn Mason

Finished size: 5½″ × 5½″

Techniques used: paints (page 6), burning (page 17), lacing (page 17), collaging (page 16)

The Lutradur was a challenge to work with, because it falls somewhere between fabric and paper. I loved how the paint was absorbed but didn't bleed, which allowed me to go crazy with my colors while still keeping a bright, unmuddied palette. The kid in me also enjoyed melting the Lutradur, and it took all my willpower to keep from watching the whole piece melt away.

—Jenn

materials

See page 62 for sources of supplies.

- Lutradur scraps
- Golden Fluid Acrylics: Quinacridone Violet, Green Gold, Cobalt Blue, Burnt Sienna
- Golden Soft Gel medium
- Found text and map paper
- Found hinge and screws
- Pigma Micron Pen (Sakura)
- Heavyweight artist paper (watercolor or printmaking work nicely)
- Butane lighter (the long kind for candles and fireplaces, not a cigarette type)
- Tongs or tweezers
- Plexiglas palette
- Paintbrush
- Painter's rags or paper towels
- Scissors
- 5" × 5" picture frame (optional)

method

See pages 6–26 for techniques.

1. With a paintbrush, cover small sections of the palette with fluid acrylic paints. Press small pieces of the Lutradur into the paint, letting some areas pick up more paint than others (page 6). Repeat on the other side of the Lutradur. Let the Lutradur pieces dry.

2. Crumple the Lutradur pieces into balls, and then open them flat. Use more fluid acrylic paints and a rag to add more color where desired. Rub the color in with the rag to get more saturation of color in random places.

3. Cut the Lutradur into the approximate shapes.

4. Using tongs or tweezers, carefully hold an ignited butane lighter under a piece of Lutradur just until the material starts to melt. Do not let it burn or the color will change.

5. Flip over the Lutradur, and melt the front as desired. You can get different depths by melting or not melting the front and back of the piece.

6. Melt around the edges of the background and the foreground where desired.

7. Add any remaining touches of fluid acrylic paints as needed to highlight the melted areas. Let the Lutradur dry completely.

8. Use the soft gel medium and a paintbrush to glue the found pieces of text to the artist paper. Cover the paper with soft gel medium, and add the prepared pieces of Lutradur. Don't press the Lutradur flat. Leave some lift to create dimension.

9. After the soft gel has dried, use the Pigma Micron Pens to add hand-drawn details.

10. Use soft gel medium to adhere the screws and the hinge. Do not move the piece until it is dry.

11. Frame as desired.

Memories of Italy

Made by Lesley Riley

Finished size: 6″ × 8″

Techniques used: paints (page 6), stencils (page 10), stamps (page 11), screening (page 12), fusing (page 19), gluing (page 18), collaging (page 16)

Lutradur is the perfect material for creating this easy folded book, because the material makes thin, sturdy pages suitable for all types of collage and embellishment. The one-piece construction format allows you the flexibility to machine sew, hand stitch, fuse, or glue your artwork to the pages. It is a great format for creating a memento of your travels, a gift for a special someone, or a commemoration of a special event in your life.

Memories of Italy is created from one rectangular piece of Lutradur that is folded into eights, creating eight sections—six pages plus the front and back covers. The book can be any size you wish. The finished book size is the same as each page size. Determine the size you want each page to be, and start with a piece of Lutradur that is four times your page width by two times your page height. For example, to make a 6″ × 8″ finished book, start with a 24″ × 16″ piece of Lutradur.

materials

See page 62 for sources of supplies.

- Lutradur: 1 piece 24″ × 16″ (to create a 6″ × 8″ book)
- Golden Fluid acrylics: Green Gold, Burnt Sienna, Quinacridone Nickel Azo Gold, Quinacridone Violet, Yellow Ochre
- Photos printed or transferred to fabric
- Rubber stamps or thermofax screens for backgrounds
- Assorted fabrics, papers, and embellishments for collaged pages
- Golden Soft Gel medium or Aleene's Fabric Fusion
- Fusible web (optional)
- Scissors or rotary cutter
- Ruler

method

See pages 6–26 for techniques.

1. Cut the Lutradur to the desired size. Paint or pattern the Lutradur (page 6), and let it dry. **Note:** Only one side of the Lutradur will show in the finished book.

2. With the wrong side of the painted Lutradur placed before you so that the rectangle is wider than it is tall, fold the Lutradur in half from top to bottom. Use the diagram at right as a guide and continue to fold it evenly 3 times from side to side, until you arrive at the finished page size. Iron to crease the folds. Open the Lutradur, and cut along the center line

between C/D and G/H (indicated by the dashed line in the diagram). Refold the pages into a book following the fold diagram. Fold the line between C and D toward you, and fold the line between G and H back away from you. Iron again to set the folds in place.

Front cover	Back cover	Page 6	Page 5
A	H	G	F
Cut along dashed line.			
B	C	D	E
Page 1	Page 2	Page 3	Page 4

Folding and layout diagram

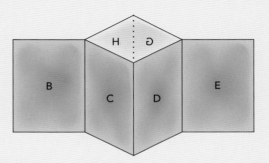

Slit cut between H/C and G/D allows you to pull pages C and D in one direction and pages G and H in opposite direction to form book. Note: Pages A and F are hidden from view.

Add art to Lutradur to create book.

3. Now it's time to create the art for your pages. Although you will only be working on one side of the opened fabric, you will need to change the orientation of the fabric before working on some of the pages so that they will be right side up when it is folded back into book form. Refer to the fold and layout diagram (page 39) for page order and layout. Page A becomes the book cover. Page H is the back cover. You will need to rotate the Lutradur to work on the covers and pages F and G.

Screen-printed text

4. Stamp, stencil, or screen backgrounds onto your pages as desired (pages 10–12). Let the Lutradur dry.

5. Sew, glue, or fuse your photos, fabrics, and embellishments to each page (pages 16, 18, 19).

6. To make your finished book, fold it in half lengthwise, so that the artwork is on the outside and pages B/C/D/E are facing you. Pull open the top of the cut section, where C/D and G/H meet to create two folds for C/D and G/H (see fold and layout diagram, page 39).

7. Push the other 2 sides of the book toward the center, forcing the fold at C/D and G/H outward. Fold A/B toward the right to create the cover and close your book. Iron the folds to set.

 If the edges of your finished book are askew after you complete your collages, adjust and sharpen the folds.

RustyCrusty

Made by Lesley Riley

Finished size: 6″ × 8″

Techniques used: paints (page 6), sealing (page 23), patinas (page 10), transfer dyes (page 9), gluing (page 18), fusing (page 19), embossing (page 20), burning (page 17), Angelina (page 23), foiling (page 24), rubbing (page 23), transferring (page 13), collaging (page 16), writing (page 21), stitching (page 16)

Rusty Crusty combines a number of techniques and is a great way to create a sample book or homage to texture. Although I started with a simple plan, every time I added another technique or texture, the book begged for more. Embossing powders are applied in a random fashion by sprinkling them over wet paint or by rubbing the Lutradur over either a clear or colored embossing pad. Small detailed areas can be created by applying paint or ink directly with a small brush or nib, and then applying the embossing powders to the Lutradur while the paint or ink is still wet.

materials

See page 62 for sources of supplies.

- Lutradur: 5 pieces each 12″ × 8″ (to create a 6″ × 8″ book)
    Extra pieces for image transfers
- Golden Fluid acrylics: Burnt Orange, Quinacridone Nickel Azo Gold, Quinacridone Violet
- Golden Soft Gel medium: matte
- Ranger ink pad and reinker: Spiced Marmalade
- Ranger embossing powders: Rust, Verdigris, Terra Cotta, Broken China
- Collage papers and fabrics
- Angelina: Forest Blaze
- Parchment paper or paper backing from fusible web
- Images printed onto inkjet transparency
- Ribbon: 1 yard for bookbinding
- Small brush or Ranger Cut n Dry nib
- Paintbrush
- Heat gun
- Chenille needle #22 or #24
- Sewing machine or hand-sewing needle
- Thread
- Clamps or clothespins (optional)

method

See pages 6–26 for techniques.

1. Paint the Lutradur pages in your chosen background colors (page 6), and let dry. Brighten and deepen the colors by sealing the painted Lutradur with a coat of matte medium (page 23).

2. Fold each page in half, and iron along the fold. Use the fold as a guide for your page artwork. Be careful not to place anything in the fold area, except on the page that will be the center spread.

3. Collage papers can be glued to the Lutradur before and after embossing (page 20). Add further embellishment with foiling, writing, and other techniques to complete your book.

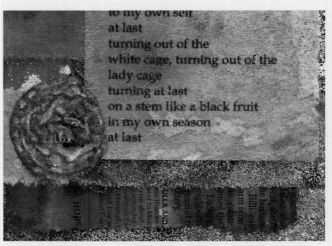

Text printed on Lutradur over embossed and collaged page

4. Apply paint or embossing inks to selected areas. Sprinkle embossing powder over wet areas. Remove the excess powders from the Lutradur, and then emboss with a heat gun (page 20). Remember to keep the heat gun 4″–5″ above the Lutradur and to use an up-and-down motion to prevent the unembossed areas from lacing or distorting.

5. Add Angelina to selected areas (page 23), and iron it onto the Lutradur using parchment paper to protect your iron. **Note:** Do not iron over any embossed areas or the embossing powders will melt again and stick to the parchment paper.

Angelina over embossed and collaged page

6. Transfer the images to Lutradur using gel medium (page 14). Cut them out, and collage to your pages.

Page-sized transferred photo on Lutradur.

7. Add more collage papers if desired, gluing or stitching in place (pages 16, 18).

8. Add any decorative stitching as desired (page 16).

9. Open all of the pages, and stack them, one on top of the other. You may wish to use clamps to hold the open stack in place while binding.

10. Thread the needle with 1 yard of ribbon. Work with the book partially folded so you can easily find the fold line. Working on the inside of the book, insert the threaded needle 3″ from the top of the book. Pull only half of the ribbon through to the outside spine, and remove the needle.

11. Return to the inside of the book. Thread the needle with the other end of the ribbon, and insert the needle into the fold 3″ above the bottom edge of the book. Pull the ribbon through to the outer spine of the book.

12. You should now have both ribbon tails on the outside of the book spine. Adjust the ribbon so that you have 2 equal lengths. Tie the ribbon, first in a knot and then, if desired, in a bow along the book spine. Add more ribbons or embellishments as desired, tying them into the binding ribbon.

Schoolhouse

Made by Lesley Riley

Finished size: 4½″ × 5¾″

Techniques used: paints (page 6), gluing (page 18), fusing (page 19), collaging (page 16)

Scrapbooking is another use for Lutradur. You can create stand-alone scrapbooks or memory books, like this one, or use it to add texture to your paper scrapbook pages. Because Lutradur holds its shape so well, I designed a schoolhouse-shaped book to hold a collection of black-and-white grade-school photos of my brothers- and sisters-in-law. The original photos are back in a framed display at my mother-in-law's house, but I now have my own set, printed on fabric and collected into this charming Lutradur book. I used scrapbook ephemera and stickers, schoolhouse print fabrics, and textbook papers to compose the collages and set the mood. The little bell in the schoolhouse roof binds the book and adds a bit of whimsy.

materials

See page 62 for sources of supplies.

- Lutradur: ¼ yard of 36"-wide Lutradur (to make 7 or 8 pages)
- Freezer paper or similar pattern paper
- Golden Fluid acrylics: Quinacridone Red, Green Gold
- Portfolio Oil Pastels
- School photos printed on paper or fabric
- School ephemera
- Fabric scraps
- Golden Soft Gel medium or Aleene's Fabric Fusion
- 2 Buttons approximately ⅜" in diameter
- Bell (optional)
- Foam brush (1")
- Scissors
- Ruler
- Hand-sewing needle
- Heavy-duty thread
- Fusible web (optional)
- Rubber stamps and inks (optional)

method

See pages 6–26 for techniques.

1. Paint the Lutradur with fluid acrylics (page 6), mixing a little green paint into red to deepen the color. Let it dry.

2. Trace the schoolhouse pattern on page 46 onto freezer paper, and cut it out. Iron the freezer paper pattern onto Lutradur as for stencils (page 10), and cut out the schoolhouse shape using the freezer paper as your guide. Repeat until you have the desired number of pages. **Note:** ¼ yard of 36"-wide Lutradur will yield exactly 8 schoolhouse pages if they are cut side by side.

3. Print your photos onto inkjet-ready fabric or paper (page 12). If desired, iron fusible web to the back of the photos printed onto fabric to prevent the fabric from fraying after cutting.

4. Add additional color to the Lutradur pages using Portfolio Oil Pastels (page 8). Add accents with rubber stamps, paint, or patterns to create fun backgrounds (pages 11, 6).

5. Gather your photos, fabric snippets, and ephemera to create a collage on each page (page 16). Glue in place. Remember to create a cover! **Note:** If photos are backed with fusible web, iron them in place.

6. Stack your finished pages together, with the cover on top. Make a large knot in the thread. Starting at the back of the stack, sew through all layers up to the top. Add a bell and button (or just a button). Sew back down through all the pages, and add another button on the back. This will prevent the stitches from pulling through the stack of pages. Stitch through the back button, up through the top button, and back down. Repeat 2 more times to secure.

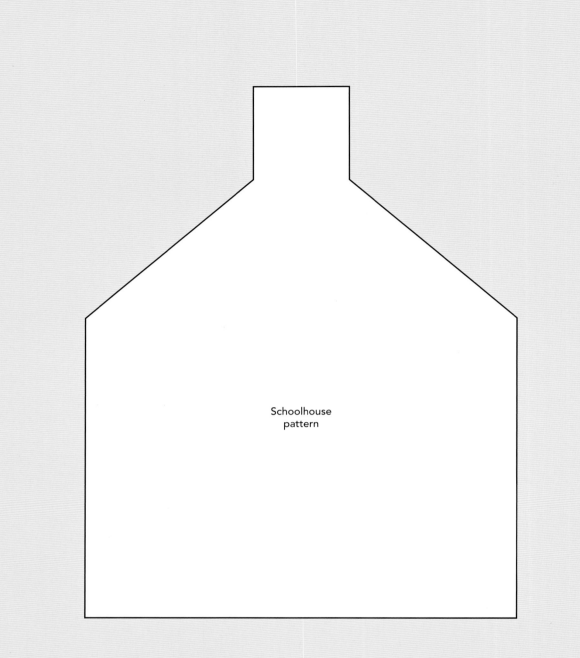

Schoolhouse
pattern

Julia

Made by Lesley Riley

Finished size: 6″ × 12″

Techniques used: paints (page 6), screening (page 12), rub-on transfers (page 15), stitching (page 16), collaging (page 16), constructing (page 22)

I have been documenting my granddaughter Julia's life in photos from the minute she was born. C&T's Ready-to-Go! 12″ × 12″ Blank Display Board Book was the starting point for this original baby book. The board book became the protective container for two fan-folded pages of painted and printed Lutradur that stand upright and spread open on display for all to see. After I added fabric, text, and a few scrapbook embellishments, Julia now has a memory book to last a lifetime... and beyond.

materials

See page 62 for sources of supplies.

- Lutradur: 2 pieces 20″ × 11½″, 1 scrap piece 8″ × 10″
- Ready-to-Go! Blank Board Book: 12″ × 12″ Display Board
- Fat quarter (or a 14″ × 14″ piece) of fabric for cover
- Golden Fluid acrylics: Quinacridone Red, Quinacridone Nickel Azo Gold
- Coordinating scrapbook paper: 1 piece 12″ × 12″
- Rubber stamps, stencil, or thermofax screen
- Gesso
- Fabric glue: Elmer's or Aleene's Easy Flow Tacky glue
- Eyelets (2 of the ⅛″ size)
- Ribbon: 1 yard ¼″ wide
- Photos and text printed on fabric or paper
- Assorted fabric scraps for collage
- Embellishments: buttons, ribbon, scrapbook stickers
- Thread
- Fiskars hole punch/eyelet setter tool
- Burnisher
- Bone folder or butter knife: to score the pages
- Chenille needle #20 or #22, or any needle that will accommodate ribbon and will fit through eyelets
- Pliers (to pull needle through book)
- Rotary mat (24″ or larger), ruler, and rotary cutter
- Sewing machine or hand-sewing needle
- Clothespins or clamps (optional)

method

See pages 6–26 for techniques.

Page Assembly

1. Paint the 2 large pieces and the scrap piece of Lutradur (page 6). Let them dry.

2. Use gesso to stamp, stencil, or screen print a pattern on one side of all the Lutradur pieces (pages 10–12). Let them dry.

3. Paint over the gesso pattern with a watery mix of Quinacridone Nickel Azo Gold and water. This will soften and blend the pattern into the background. Let it dry.

4. Measure, score, and fan-fold the 2 larger pieces of Lutradur at the following intervals: 5½″, 4¾″, 4¼″, 3¼″, 2¼″. Iron the folds in place.

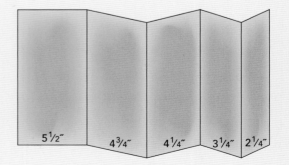

Fold diagram for right-side pages. Reverse to create left-side pages.

Completed fan-folded pages open for display

 Scoring creates a line or depression in the Lutradur that will help it fold. Scoring is most often done with a bone folder, but any blunt edge, such as a butter knife, will work. Line up the ruler on the fold line to be scored. (Score on the outside *edge of the intended fold.) Run the tool down the line, along the edge of the ruler.*

5. Open up the folded Lutradur, and create the page art. The two 5½"-wide pages will become the 2 centermost pages. The smallest 2¼" pages will become the tabs that you use to open out the fanfolds. Create a collage on each page. Glue, hand stitch, or machine stitch your collage in place. On the two 5½"-wide pages, leave a ¼" margin on the outside edge for attaching the binding strip.

 Do not place anything on a fold unless you want it to fold over onto the next page.

6. Cut a 2" × 9" binding strip from the scrap piece of Lutradur. Fold it in half lengthwise. Place an eyelet 1" from the top and just to the right of the fold. Place the second eyelet 1" from the bottom edge and just to the left of the fold. (This placement allows the book to fold closed evenly.) Center the binding strip lengthwise between the 2 pages, placing ½" of the strip under each edge. Pin. Stitch in place with a ¼" seam.

Binding strip

Cover Assembly

1. Fold the scrapbook paper in half. With the board book open flat, spread a thin, even coat of white glue inside the board book. Place the folded edge of the scrapbook paper into the book's fold, where there is a slight indentation. Hold up the left side of the board book, and burnish the fold of the scrapbook paper into the fold of the book. Working from the center out to the book's edge, smooth the right side of the scrapbook paper over the board book. Repeat on the left side.

A little glue goes a long way. If you use too much glue, it will soak through your fabric. My rule is if you can see the white of the glue, you are using too much. Be sure to spread a thin, even layer. Any areas of fabric not glued down will create puckers.

2. Fold in 1″ along the top and bottom edges of the cover fabric to create a piece that is 12″ × 14″. Iron the folds, and glue or stitch them in place. (The extra 2″ at the side edges of the fabric are needed to accommodate the spine of the book and to create attractive folded edges on the inside of the book.) For a raw-edge finish, cut the cover fabric to 12¼″ × 13½″.

3. To ensure that the cover art is centered on the cover fabric, fold the cover fabric over the book, and temporarily mark the portion of fabric that will become the front cover. I like to use straight pins or chalk. Create the cover art, check its placement, and then glue or stitch the art in place.

4. Place the cover fabric right side down on a flat surface. Spread an even layer of glue on the back of the book cover only. Line up of the back of the book with the top, bottom, and side of the fabric, leaving a ½″ allowance on each side for folding over the edge. Working from the edge toward the spine, smooth the fabric in place. Spread glue on the book spine and front cover. With the book in the closed position, smooth the cover fabric, from the spine toward the front cover.

5. Spread glue along the inside edges of the book cover. Fold over the fabric, and glue in place. You can clamp it with clothespins until the glue is dry.

Finishing

1. Thread a needle with 1 yard of ribbon. Work with the book partially folded, so you can position the fold of the binding strip in the fold of the book. Center the pages and binding strip inside the book cover. Clamp them in place if desired.

Insert the threaded needle into the top eyelet, and push it through the book spine. Use pliers to pull the needle through the spine. Pull only half of the ribbon through to the front. Remove the needle from the ribbon.

2. Open the book, and thread the other end of the ribbon through the needle. Repeat Step 1 to attach the lower eyelet to the spine.

3. You should now have both ribbon tails on the outside of the book spine. Adjust the ribbon so that you have 2 equal lengths. Tie the ribbon, first in a knot and then in a bow along the book spine.

Aviary

Made by Lesley Riley
Finished size: 22″ × 32″
Techniques used: transferring (page 13), paints (page 6), burning (page 17),
stitching (page 16), fusing (page 19), collaging (page 16)

Lutradur-transferred birds perched on Lutradur branches gather in a forest of fabrics. A fascination with birds and their accoutrements—nests, eggs, feathers, and wings—has been providing artists, writers, and bird aficionados with inspiration for centuries. The more than 9,000 species of birds offer an almost unlimited source of material and images to draw from. Lured by their vibrant colors and the charm of antique illustrations, I made this mixed-media quilt to satisfy a part of my bird lust. I chose fabrics with a woodland theme in mind. By transferring the bird images onto Lutradur, I was able to keep their intense, bright color and cut them out without worrying about fraying edges. The addition of Lutradur branches gives just the right amount of texture and dimension to this menagerie of winged creatures.

materials

See page 62 for sources of supplies.

- Lutradur: 1 piece approximately 8″ × 20″ for bird transfers
    1 piece 6″ × 12″ for branches
- Coordinating fabric: 10–12 strips, each approximately 6″ × 20″
- Fabric for sky: 12″ × 20″
- Fabric for one-piece backing and borders: approximately 28″ × 38″
- Batting: 22″ × 32″
- Bird images (available from www.lesleyriley.com)
- Inkjet transparencies
- Golden Soft Gel medium: matte
- Paper-backed fusible web
- Foam brush (1″)
- Burnisher
- Heat tool for cutting branches
- Sewing machine

method

See pages 6–26 for techniques.

1. Transfer the bird images onto the larger piece of Lutradur (page 14). Cut out the images.

2. Paint the smaller piece of Lutradur brown, and let it dry. Use a heat tool to carve branch shapes from brown-painted Lutradur (page 17).

3. To create the raw-edged appliquéd background, use the batting as your work surface. Cut or tear fabric strips to create a sky and forest, overlapping the fabrics from the top to the bottom, starting with the sky. Lightly tack the strips in place by placing strips of fusible web (paper removed) between both the overlapping fabric strips and the batting. Iron for 2 seconds with a dry iron. **Do not fuse the strips to the batting.** Alternately, you can strip piece your background for a clean-edged appearance.

4. Slowly peel the fused top away from the batting, trim the edges even, and set aside. Determine the border width you would like for the quilt, and create a package-fold quilt (see Appendix, page 61) from your chosen backing/border fabric and the batting. Center the quilt top over the quilt sandwich, and iron to fuse in place, following the manufacturer's directions for fusing.

5. Starting in the middle of the quilt where the forest meets the sky, stitch the fabric strips through all 3 layers, working toward the bottom.

6. Place the birds on the quilt top, and pin or tack them in place by placing bits of fusible web (paper removed) between the birds and the quilt top. Iron for 2 seconds. Pin the branches to the quilt top. Stitch the birds and branches in place.

7. Add additional hand or machine quilting as desired.

Angelic

Made by Lesley Riley

Finished size: 17½″ × 27″

Techniques used: transferring (page 13), paints (page 6), lacing (page 17), foiling (page 24), burning (page 17), fusing (page 19), stitching (page 16), layering (page 22), collaging (page 16)

This quilt is my homage to the ornate, gilded surfaces that contrasted with the worn, faded beauty of the frescoes I saw in churches on my first (and I hope not my last) trip to Italy in 2007. The angel image, one of a large personal collection, is from a local cemetery. Lutradur is an excellent surface for creating real and faux textures as well as the look of ancient peeling surfaces. Art quilts are the perfect showcase for Lutradur's variety of talents. There are few materials you can work with to achieve both an ornate and a crumbling, aged appearance.

Find inspiration in a decorative pattern from your travels or from print or online resources. Dover Publications has an extensive library of patterns in both inexpensive books and on CD.

materials

See page 62 for sources of supplies.

- Lutradur:
  1 piece 14" × 19"
  1 piece 5½" × 5½"
  1 piece 4" × 4" for image transfer
- Coordinating fabric:
  2 pieces 18" × 27½" for pillow quilt top and backing
  4 pieces 3½" × 3½" to 10" × 11" to frame angel image
- Contrasting fabric 1: 1 piece 13" × 20" to go behind laced, stenciled Lutradur
- Contrasting fabric 2: 1 piece 14" × 22" to layer under the first contrasting fabric
- Batting: 18" × 27½"
- Paper-backed fusible web:
  1 piece 6" × 12" or large enough to cover stencil area
  2 pieces 2" × 17"
  2 pieces 2" × 24"
- Angel image printed on inkjet transparency
- Decorative stencil pattern, measuring approximately 12" × 5"
- Acrylic paint
- Golden Soft Gel medium: matte
- Lumiere paint: Bright Gold
- Jones Tones Foil: copper, gold
- Heat tool such as the Creative Textile Tool
- Cookie sheet or heat-resistant surface
- Heat gun
- Small, round-tipped brush
- Iron
- Foam brush (1")
- Burnisher

method

See pages 6–26 for techniques.

1. Paint the 14" × 19" and 5½" × 5½" pieces of Lutradur the colors of your choice. Let them dry.

2. Transfer the angel image to the 4" × 4" piece of Lutradur (page 13), and cut it out. Use a small, round-tipped brush to paint the edges of the image with gold Lumiere (page 6).

3. Use the heat gun to lace the 5½" × 5½" piece of Lutradur (page 17). Prepare the Lutradur for foiling by ironing fusible web over the Lutradur, and then iron the foil in place (page 24). Crumple the sheet of foil before ironing it to the areas of the Lutradur covered with fusible web. Protect your iron by placing parchment or release paper (the paper backing from the fusible web) between the foil, the fusible web, and the

iron. Use the edge of your iron to iron the foil to the Lutradur. Do not try for complete coverage.

4. Place the 3½" × 3½" fabric behind the angel image, and layer onto the laced Lutradur.

5. Create 3 frames for the image from layers of graduated sizes of coordinating fabrics.

6. When the angel collage is complete, place it on the 14" × 19" piece of painted Lutradur. Determine the positioning for the decorative stencil. Set the collage aside.

7. Tape the stencil pattern behind the Lutradur, and trace it onto the Lutradur with a pencil. Remove the pattern.

8. With the traced pattern as your guide, use the heat tool to cut out the stencil pattern (page 17). Don't worry about being exact or totally symmetrical, as you will be distorting the work later.

9. Prepare the Lutradur for foiling by ironing fusible web over both the cut stencil area and the exposed sides of the Lutradur that the angel collage will not cover (page 24). Remove the paper backing.

10. Crumple the sheet of foil before ironing it to the areas of the Lutradur covered with fusible web. Protect your iron by placing parchment or release paper (the paper backing from the fusible web) between the foil, the fusible web, and the iron. Use the edge of your iron to iron the foil to the cut stencil and to other prepared areas of the Lutradur. Do not try for complete coverage.

11. Distort the foiled and cut stencil areas with a heat gun. Lightly lace the surrounding area and all 4 edges of the entire Lutradur piece.

12. To add further highlights and accents, use the small brush to paint the cut edges of the stencil with gold paint.

13. Stitch the angel collage to the Lutradur. Stitch the Lutradur to the 2 contrasting fabrics (page 16).

14. Create a pillow quilt for your angel collage (see Appendix, page 61).

15. Place your stitched Lutradur collage on top of the pillow quilt, and hand or machine stitch in place though all the layers.

16. Add additional quilting as desired.

Let's Play

Made by Lesley Riley
Finished size: 20½″ × 34½″
Techniques used: paints (page 6), transferring (page 13), layering (page 22),
writing (page 21), fusing (page 19), stitching (page 16)

It is not unusual for a photograph in my collection to inspire a quilt. Using my scanner and Adobe Photoshop, I was able to enlarge the photo, print it onto four inkjet transparencies, and transfer it onto one large piece of lamé to create the effect that the girl is sitting on a sliding board. I then appliquéd this central image onto a quilt top created from one large piece of painted Lutradur. I enhanced the appliqué by drawing in the other parts of the sliding board. A hopscotch pattern and the invitation to play were both transferred directly from transparencies onto the Lutradur.

Finding just the right fabric to peek out from underneath the translucent quilt top was a fun challenge. I realized that I could change the mood, the message, and, most of all, the overall appearance of the whole quilt, just by deciding what to place under the Lutradur. The art of layering!

The dimensions I chose related to the size of the photo I used. Adjust your overall quilt dimensions based on the photo you choose.

materials

See page 62 for sources of supplies.

- Lutradur: approximately 24" × 34"
- Fabric: 2 pieces 21" × 35" for quilt top and backing
- Lamé (or fabric of your choice): 1 piece approximately 15" × 24" (optional)
- Batting: 21" × 35"*
- Golden Fluid acrylics: Manganese blue, Quinacridone Nickel Azo Gold
- Images printed on inkjet transparencies
- Golden Soft Gel medium: matte
- Foam brush (1")
- Sharpie marker
- Rotary cutter, mat, and ruler
- Decorative blade for the rotary cutter (optional)

* Use felt, flannel, or Warm & Natural batting to prevent any migration of fibers through the open webbing of the Lutradur quilt top.

method

See pages 6–26 for techniques.

1. Paint the 24" × 34" piece of Lutradur (page 6), and let it dry. Trim it to approximately 18½" × 31½". **Note:** Use a rotary cutter with a decorative edge for a unique look.

2. Transfer the image to the lamé or fabric of your choice (page 13). Let it dry, iron the image onto fusible web, and then cut it out.

 To work with lamé, stabilize it by ironing fusible web to the back before cutting or transferring an image onto it.

3. Decide on the position of the central image, and fuse it in place.

4. Transfer additional text or images directly to the Lutradur quilt top.

5. Use a Sharpie marker to add additional drawings, words, and so forth.

6. Finish the quilt, using one of the methods in the Appendix (page 61).

 Because the Lutradur is somewhat transparent, using a light fabric behind a Lutradur quilt top produces the brightest finished quilt. Experiment with different colors to create other layered effects. Don't stop there! What about layering dictionary pages, other fabric snippets, or more photos, to name a few options?

Oh the Places I've Been

Made by Lesley Riley

Finished size: 22″ × 22″

Techniques used: paints (page 6), resists (page 21), lacing (page 17), layering (page 22), collaging (page 16)

The year 2007 was when my art took me places I never imagined I'd see—New Zealand, Australia, both the Indian Ocean and the South Pacific, Italy, and the Grand Canyon. I documented my presence in these amazing places by photographing my feet—in water, on lava rock, against Italian marble, and over the edges of cliffs. Step into my world for a moment.

Nine photos were printed onto fabric and stitched together, with their delicate, painted, paper towel frames, onto a sheet of painted Lutradur. The stitched photos masked the Lutradur, the exposed areas of which were laced with a heat gun. This style created a stable yet delicate-looking background. With the dark brown and the matching blue of the background fabric peeking through the laced Lutradur, I was able to create contrast, depth, and dimension with just two layers.

Creating depth and dimension with layering

materials

See page 62 for sources of supplies.

- Lutradur: 15″ × 15″
- Fabric: 1 piece 32″ × 32″ for border/backing of the quilt
    1 piece 16½″ × 16½″ for center background
- Batting: 22″ × 22″
- Golden Fluid Acrylics
- Pretreated or inkjet-ready fabric (regular or fusible): 1 sheet
- Paper-backed fusible web (if not using inkjet fabric that is already backed)
- Fabric or paper: approximately 12″ × 12″ total to frame photos
- Paint brush
- Heat gun

method

See pages 6–26 for techniques.

1. Paint the Lutradur (page 6) and paper. Let them dry.

2. Use a computer to size your photos to approximately 2″ × 2″. Print the photos onto inkjet-ready fabric, back with a fusible web (if not already backed), and trim to create a narrow white frame around each photo.

3. Cut fabric or paper frames 3″ × 3″ to back each photo. Iron the photos to fuse them to the frames.

4. Pin each photo/frame onto the Lutradur in a grid pattern and stitch in place (page 16).

5. With your heat gun, lace the Lutradur around the edges and between the photos (page 17).

6. Create a package-fold quilt using the backing/border fabric and batting (see Appendix, page 61).

7. Center the Lutradur and background fabric on the quilt sandwich.

8. Stitch around the Lutradur and zigzag stitch around the edges of the background fabric. Add other quilting as desired.

Autumn Field

Made by Lesley Riley
Finished size: 8″ × 12″ felted piece, 12″ × 17″ quilt
Techniques used: paints (page 6), needle felting (page 26), stitching (page 16)

materials

See page 62 for sources of supplies.

- Lutradur: approximately 12″ × 16″
- Wool and silk fibers and yarns: autumn and field colors
- Needle felting machine or attachment, or hand felting needle
- Fabric: 2 pieces 12½″ × 17½″ for front and back of pillow quilt
  1 piece approximately 9½″ × 14½″ for background
- Batting: 12½″ × 17½″
- Acrylic paints
- Brushes
- Silk leaves for embellishment (purchased at a craft store)

method

See pages 6–26 for techniques.

1. Paint the Lutradur (page 6). Let it dry.

2. Using a pencil, lightly sketch areas or shapes you want to felt onto the Lutradur.

3. Use a needle felting machine or hand felting needle to do the felting (page 26).

4. Trim the finished felted Lutradur to approximately 8″ × 12″.

5. Create a pillow quilt (see Appendix, page 61).

6. Stitch the background fabric and felted Lutradur to the finished pillow quilt. Add additional quilting as desired.

7. Arrange the leaves, and sew them on by stitching through the center of each leaf.

Appendix

Easy Quilt Finishing Methods

These simple quilt finishing techniques will provide borders, finished edges, and a backing for your quilt top—all in one easy step.

Package-Fold Finish

This is a simple and time-saving method that uses the quilt backing fabric to create a finished edge and borders for your quilt—all at the same time.

1. Determine the size of the backing fabric by measuring the size of the finished quilt top and adding the width of the desired borders on all 4 sides. Then add another 4″ to that measurement (2″ per side seam allowance).

2. Cut the batting to the size of the finished quilt (quilt top plus borders).

3. Place the backing fabric right side down.

4. Center the batting on the quilt backing.

5. Fold the 2 long sides of the backing fabric over the batting edge toward the quilt center. Iron. Fold the 2 short sides toward the center, turning the corners in at a 45° angle and mitering the corners as if you were wrapping a package.

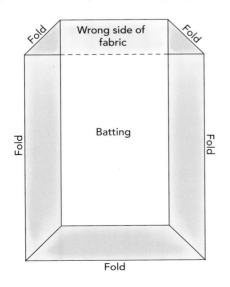

6. Trim any excess fabric from the mitered corners, and iron flat.

7. Center the quilt top onto the batting/backing sandwich. The quilt top should cover the batting as well as the extra 2″ of the folded-in edges of the backing. Pin or baste in place, or stitch around all 4 edges of the quilt top to secure it to the batting and backing.

8. Machine or hand quilt through all 3 layers in a pattern of your choice.

9. To accentuate the border, stitch around the quilt ¼″ from the edge of the quilt. If desired, repeat the edge stitching ¼″ from your first line.

Pillow Finish

This quilt finish is made just like you would cover a pillow: Sew all four sides, leaving an opening for turning it inside out. This pillow provides a great surface for collage work and is an easy way to finish edges.

1. Measure your finished quilt top, and then determine the size of the borders that you want around your finished quilt top. Add the border widths to the finished measurement of the quilt top plus ½″ seam allowance.

2. Cut 2 pieces of fabric and 1 piece of batting to the measured size. Place the 2 pieces of fabric right sides together on top of the batting. Pin the edges together. Leave an opening of 4″ or more on one edge for turning the quilt sandwich inside out. Use a ¼″ seam allowance to stitch around all 4 edges, except for the 4″ opening.

3. Trim the excess batting at the stitched line. Trim the corners at a 45° angle.

4. Turn the quilt sandwich inside out, and poke out the corners. Iron the edges of the pillow quilt flat. Hand stitch the opening closed.

5. Center the quilt top on top of the quilt pillow. Pin or baste in place.

6. Stitch around all 4 edges to secure the top to the pillow. Add any additional quilting as desired.

Resources

Most of the products mentioned in this book are available at your local or online art, craft, stamp, quilt, or fabric store. If you are not familiar with a product, it's helpful to look at it online first, so that you know what you are looking for or exactly what to ask for. For more product information and to order the more unique products directly from the manufacturer (indicated with an asterisk), visit their website.

ONLINE RESOURCES FOR SCREEN PRINTING

wikiHow: How to Do Screen Printing on Fabric—www.wikiHow.com/Do-Screen-Printing-on-Fabric

EZScreenPrint—www.ezscreenprint.com

Thermofax Silk-Screen Printing—www.friendsfabricart.com/Free-Articles/Thermofax-Printing.html

Thermofax Screens—www.thermofaxscreens.co.uk/faq.html

BOOKS FOR SCREEN PRINTING

Complex Cloth: A Comprehensive Guide to Surface Design by Jane Dunnewold, Martingale and Company, 1996

Screenprinting: The Complete Water-Based System by Robert Adam and Carol Robertson, Thames & Hudson, 2004

Simple Screenprinting: Basic Techniques & Creative Projects by Annie Stromquist, Lark Books, 2005

The Surface Designer's Handbook: Dyeing, Printing, Painting, and Creating Resists on Fabric by Holly Brackmann, Interweave Press, 2006

SOURCES FOR SUPPLIES

Listed alphabetically by product or product name

AccuCut die-cutting machine—www.accucut.com

Aleene's glues—www.duncancrafts.com

*Angel images CD—www.lesleyriley.com

Basic Grey rub-ons—www.basicgrey.com

Beacon adhesives (including Fabri-Tac, Gem-Tac)—www.beaconadhesives.com

*Bird images CD—www.lesleyriley.com

Bubble Jet Set—www.cjenkinscompany.com

Caran D'Ache water-soluble crayons—www.carandache.ch

*Cat's eye stickers—www.lasioux.com

Charms—www.artgirlz.com

Creative Textile Tool—www.walnuthollow.com

Cricut and Cuttlebug die-cut—www.provocrafts.com

Diamond Glaze—www.diamondglaze.com

Distress inks—www.rangerink.com

Dover Design Library—www.doverpublications.com

Dye-na-Flow—www.jacquard.com

Embossing pen and powders—www.rangerink.com

Eyelets and eyelet setter/hole punch tool—www.fiskars.com

EZ Walnut Ink and TintZ—www.fiberscraps.com

Fibers for felting—www.quiltingarts.com

Foil paper—www.jonestones.com

Freezer paper—your local grocery store

Golden Fluid Acrylics, Golden Matte, and Golden Soft Gel Medium—www.goldenpaints.com

Heat gun—www.uchida.com

Inkjet-ready fabric—www.electricquilt.com or www.colortextiles.com

Iron—www.clover-usa.com

Jacquard Textile Color—www.jacquard.com

Krylon Easy-Tack Repositionable Adhesive—www.krylon.com

Lumiere paint—www.jacquard.com

Lutradur—www.lesleyriley.com or www.shoppellon.com

Me & My Big Ideas iron-ons—www.meandmybigideas.com

Mica—www.usartquest.com

Mylar—local craft and art supply stores

Needle felting machine and attachments—www.babylock.com, www.janome.com, or www.bernina.com

Needle felting tool—www.clover-usa.com

Parchment paper—Grocery store

Patina paints—www.patina.com

Pigma Micron Pens—www.sakuraofamerica.com

Pigment inks—www.rangerink.com

Portfolio Oil Pastels (Crayola)—www.portfolioseries.com

*PYMII—www.precision-blue.com

Ready-to-Go! Blank Board Blocks and Blank Board Books—www.ctpub.com

Setacolor paint—www.pebeo.com/us

Screen printing—www.photoez.com or www.cbridge.com

Shiva Paintstiks—www.dharmatrading.com or www.lauramurraydesigns.com

Simply foam stamps—www.plaidonline.com

Sizzix die-cuts—www.sizzix.com

Speedball calligraphy ink—www.speedballart.com

StazOn inks—www.tsukineko.com

Stretched canvas—www.fredrixartistcanvas.com

*Transfer Artist paper—www.transferartist.com

Transfer dyes—www.prochemical.com (see directions for use at www.prochemical.com/directions/ProsperseTransferPrinting.htm)

Transparencies—local office supply stores or www.business-supply.com

Tulip Soft Fabric paint—www.duncancrafts.com

UTEE—www.rangerink.com

Warm & Natural batting—www.warmcompany.com

Wonder-Under fusible—www.shoppellon.com

*Wool felt cone, wool felt beads, die-cuts—www.artgirlz.com

Available only through these suppliers

For a list of other fine books from C&T Publishing, ask for a free catalog:
C&T Publishing, Inc.
P.O. Box 1456
Lafayette, CA 94549
(800) 284-1114
Email: ctinfo@ctpub.com
Website: www.ctpub.com

C&T Publishing's professional photography services are now available to the public. Visit us at www.ctmediaservices.com.

For quilting supplies:
Cotton Patch
1025 Brown Ave.
Lafayette, CA 94549
Store: (925) 284-1177
Mail order: (925) 283-7883
Email: CottonPa@aol.com
Website: www.quiltusa.com

Note: Fabrics used in the projects shown may not be currently available, as fabric manufacturers keep most fabrics in print for only a short time.

About the Author

Best known for her Fragment series of small fabric collages, Lesley Riley is an internationally known teacher, author, quilter, and mixed-media artist who has a passion for color and the written word. Her work takes the form of art quilts, fabric books, dolls, and more. Lesley's art and articles have appeared in numerous publications, and her work has been in juried shows and is held in many private collections.

In her first book, *Quilted Memories,* Lesley brought new ideas and techniques to quilting and preserving memories. Her second book, *Fabric Memory Books,* combined fabric and innovative ideas with the art of bookmaking. As contributing editor of *Cloth Paper Scissors* magazine, Lesley regularly shares her latest ideas and techniques in the magazine. Through her website (www.lesleyriley.com), Lesley aspires to inspire others to find their own voice and to share in the magic that is art.

When not teaching, writing about, or making art, Lesley, a Washington, D.C. native, loves spending time with her high-school sweetheart husband, six children, and five granddaughters.

Contributors

Claudine Hellmuth—www.claudinehellmuth.com
    claudine@collageartist.com
Judi Kauffmann—judineedle@aol.com
Katie Kendrick—www.joyouslybecoming.typepad.com
    joyouslybecoming@earthlink.net
Jenn Mason—www.jennmason.com
    jennmason@jennmason.com

Great Titles
from C&T PUBLISHING

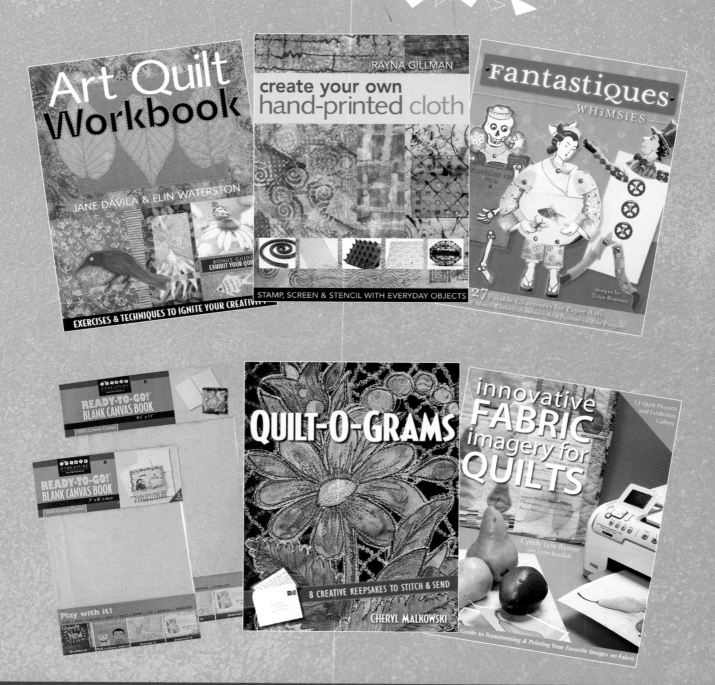

Art Quilt Workbook
JANE DÁVILA & ELIN WATERSTON
BONUS GUIDE
EXHIBIT YOUR QUILTS
EXERCISES & TECHNIQUES TO IGNITE YOUR CREATIVITY

RAYNA GILLMAN
create your own hand-printed cloth
STAMP, SCREEN & STENCIL WITH EVERYDAY OBJECTS

Fantastiques WHiMSiES
27 Posable Characters for Paper Arts
& Match Embellishments • Add Fantasy to Any Project
designs by Trice Boerens

READY-TO-GO! BLANK CANVAS BOOK 8½" x 11"
100% Cotton Canvas
READY-TO-GO! BLANK CANVAS BOOK 7" x 8" 2-PACK
100% Cotton Canvas
Play with it!

QUILT-O-GRAMS
8 CREATIVE KEEPSAKES TO STITCH & SEND
CHERYL MALKOWSKI

innovative FABRIC imagery for QUILTS
13 Quilt Projects and Exhibition Gallery
Cyndy Lyle Rymer with Lynn Koolish
Guide to Transforming & Printing Your Favorite Images on Fabric